Working with
Multiproblem Families

Working with Multiproblem Families

Lisa Kaplan
Northeastern Family Institute

Lexington Books
D.C. Heath and Company/Lexington, Massachusetts/Toronto

Library of Congress Cataloging-in-Publication Data

Kaplan, Lisa.
  Working with multiproblem families.

  Includes index.
  1. Family social work—United States.   2. Problem
families—Counseling of—United States.   I. Title.
HV699.K36   1986   362.8′25323′0973   85–45010
ISBN 0–669–13210–1 (alk. paper)
ISBN 0–669–11097–3 (pbk. : alk. paper)

Published simultaneously in Canada
Printed in the United States of America
Casebound International Standard Book Number: 0–669–13210–1
Paperbound International Standard Book Number: 0–669–11097–3
Library of Congress Catalog Card Number: 85–45010

The paper used in this publication meets the minimum requirements of American National
Standard for Information Sciences—Permanence of Paper for Printed Library Materials, ANSI
Z39.48–1984.

The last numbers on the right below indicate the number and date of printing.

10 9 8 7 6 5 4 3

95 94 93 92 91 90 89 88 87

To *Judy Chandler*

Contents

Foreword

Yitzhak Bakal
Northeastern Family Institute

For several decades the attention of theoreticians, researchers, and workers in the field of human services has focused on two important developments: deinstitutionalization and the field of family therapy. These developments were, and still are, growing and moving in parallel directions, with few attempts either in theory or practice to integrate them. This book succeeds in merging these two developments.

The field of family therapy has made a tremendous contribution to the exploration of the family as a social system. Workers in the fields of social services, psychology, and psychiatry have greatly benefited from insights gained from such exploration. The emphasis in theory and practice has centered almost exclusively on the middle class, the motivated, and single-problem families. The family issues of the working class with its multiple problems and needs, have remained out of the scope of interest of researchers and practitioners. Paradoxically, it is these families who are most in need of help. Moreover, help given has often exacerbated their problems. Public bureaucracies in charge of helping these families have labeled them, increased their dependency, and made them less equipped to deal with their own children. Often, the process of help itself has become "the problem." In describing her negative experiences, one mother said, "When the authorities decided to place one of my children because of my alcohol problems, it confirmed my worst fears; that I am not fit to be a mother." This is a vicious cycle. People who are failing often receive help that only aggravates and complicates their problems.

The field of institutional care created similar concerns and dilemmas. Children and adults were warehoused in large settings that further labeled them and, in the name of help, took away their dignity, rendering them more dependent and ill equipped to deal with their family life situations. It is evident that large institutions and state hospitals are not solutions, but strong contributors to their problems.

Deinstitutionalization is an attempt to answer these concerns. The closing of institutions in Massachusetts and the diversion of people from state hospitals and youth correctional facilities in the sixties and seventies opened a new and important chapter of hope for both clients and practitioners in the field of human services.

The mother I quoted earlier had three of seven children incarcerated in institutions. She lost support of a husband, began to fail as a mother in controlling and attending to her children's growing problems and needs, and turned to alcohol. She received "help" from community agencies, who took the children away, further confirming her failure and helplessness. Similar processes occurred in the institutions in dealing with these children's problems. One of these youths "graduated" to adult corrections through his association with other delinquents he met at the institution. The other two returned home, posing a new set of problems for their mother and the local authorities.

Deinstitutionalization succeeded in combating the "out of sight, out of mind" approach to those who failed in their homes and communities. It also forced new options to be found that were more humane, less destructive, and less costly. Whether these new alternatives are group homes, community residences, or foster care placements, they are superior to the institution. They resemble the home and provide the atmosphere and skills necessary to survive in the community. Despite their superiority, they still have one thing in common with the institutional setting: they are artificial and temporary establishments that can neither replace the family nor replicate the "real" community. Research has shown that a very high percentage of out-of-home placements, whether they are children or adolescents placed in foster homes or institutional settings, return to their own homes. No matter how destructive, punishing, or chaotic the home environment is, it has a strong attraction.

Deinstitutionalization forces us to further explore and find ways to strengthen and build families, especially families who are poor and disenfranchised. This excellent book provides detailed descriptions of successful programs that work with multiproblem families, and recommends a comprehensive program model. It also gives us a very useful set of principles and a conceptual framework for initiating and maintaining such programs.

Preface and Acknowledgments

This book evolved as a result of my work with multiproblem families. Although I was trained as a family therapist, I found that most family therapy literature failed to consider multiproblem families. Many agencies continue to employ treatment strategies which focus on the individual and neglect the family. I wrote this book to fill the gap. I provide the reader with a framework for working with multiproblem families. The annotated bibliography encourages further exploration. My book is only a beginning. Much more work and research needs to be done for these heretofore neglected families.

The vignettes are drawn from cases I have worked with over the years. The names have been changed and situations altered to protect the privacy of the families.

Many people contributed, directly and indirectly, to this book. Dr. Carol Peacock urged me to seek publication. Dr. Martin Bloom, as always, supported my efforts. Judy Chandler and Ron Morin's excitement about my ideas and constant encouragement were invaluable. I have always admired Judy's personal strength and courage, which have gotten her where she is today. Her commitment and success in working with multiproblem families is meritorious. I especially appreciate the long hours Judy spent with me, debating various concepts. I am indebted to Ron for his dedicated editing, ongoing assistance, and inexhaustible patience. His continuous enthusiasm and support are greatly appreciated.

I want to thank Dr. Baruch Shulem and Eric Emery who, long ago, encouraged my interest in family therapy. I also want to thank my family; friends, especially Melvin Carlson and Kris Brown; and the staff at Northeastern Family Institute and Community Program Innovations for their interest and support. Dr. Yitzhak Bakal, Executive Director of Northeastern Family Institute, and the staff of Brockton's Comprehensive Counseling Program, through their commitment to working with multiproblem families, gave me the opportunity to explore this area in depth. I also want to thank Marjorie Peskin for her IBM connection, Arthur Goldhammer for his hardware and software expertise, and Susan Holbert for preparing my index. The library at Boston College School of Social Work provided the resources I needed, and the librarians took a special interest in my book.

Through my work, I was fortunate to meet a number of exciting individuals who went out of their way for me. Al Herbert of the Lower East Side Family Union provided me with an understanding of his program and took a genuine interest in my work. Ed Hinckley of Maine Department of Mental Health and Mental Retardation went out of his way to meet with me, provided extensive material about Maine's home-based services, and contributed his expertise and experience. Beulah Compton of the University of Alabama gave me further insight into the St. Paul Family Centered Project. I corresponded with and visited a number of family preservation programs, many of which I was regrettably unable to include in my book. I appreciate the time and effort of the individuals representing these programs; their assistance was invaluable.

Most of all, I want to thank the families.

Introduction

Preserving the family must become the guiding philosophical principle of the social service profession; a family is best served when it is preserved as a family. Although legal mandates and agency philosophies express a commitment to family preservation, in actuality, the family is treated with little respect. Placement is commonly used; it is easier to place than assist a family in reconstituting itself. The philosophical underpinnings of the human service profession must undergo a total reorientation if commitment to family preservation is to become reality.

Multiproblem families have received little attention. Literature specifically focusing on this population is scarce, leaving the practitioner with few theories and little hard data to guide diagnostic inquiry, treatment strategies, and delivery of effective services. Too often, social service agencies force multiproblem families into time-honored conceptual frameworks in an attempt to understand and treat the symptoms presented. Traditional treatment strategies, however, fail to meet the needs of this population.[1]

The social service delivery systems of most states compartmentalize service provision; individuals are classified according to the problems they present. People are labeled and treated according to the categories assigned to them. "Most clinical theorists, planners, and practitioners, regardless of discipline, seem caught in the highly specialized sequence of their own training and intradisciplinary experience, upon which they seem to depend for the very definition of their personal identity."[2] This observation indicates the negative aspects of the specialization and fragmentation in the field of psychology. For example, the Department of Alcoholism treats only those with alcohol problems; the Department of Drug Rehabilitation treats only those with drug problems; the Department of Mental Health serves only those with mental health problems. Such thinking is linear rather than systemic. There is little concern for the individual as a whole, and services seldom focus on the family of the individual.[3] In addition, state agencies often work at odds with one another. It is not unusual for a person to be sent from one agency to another in search of services.

In various parts of the country a quiet, little-publicized movement toward the provision of home-based, family-centered services is growing, with assistance from organizations attempting to unify the effort. Despite small advances, the use of in-home family services as a treatment alternative remains little understood. For the most part, the movement is completely outside the traditional social service delivery system. In theory, the child welfare system is committed to maintaining children in their own homes; yet, in practice, placement is the treatment most often employed.[4] In many communities, there are no home-based, family-centered services, and placement is the only treatment option available.

In the past, placement was used extensively, without question. Quality and efficacy of care was of little concern; alternatives to placement were not even a consideration. Since the 1950s, however, the effectiveness of out-of-home placement has been challenged. Many researchers indicate the drawbacks of institutionalization and foster care, while some point to the negative and often irreparable effects of such placement.[5] We, as professionals, abandon parents or allow parents to abandon their children. Instead, we must preserve a child's connection to the family, balancing the need to protect the child with the need to keep the family together. Maintaining parental involvement is crucial.

The United States has no national commitment to keep families together. Other countries have strong family preservation policies; our country does not. Child welfare services are based on the belief that intervention should occur only when a family can no longer provide for its child(ren). Bronfenbrenner maintains that U.S. public policies are detrimental because they employ a deficit model. "To qualify for help, potential recipients must first prove that they and their families are inadequate — they must do so in writing, a dozen times over, with corroborating documentation, so that there can be little doubt that they are in fact the inadequate persons they say they are."[6] We must develop a national policy that recognizes the importance of the family and promotes positive family life. This policy must transfer power from patronizing social service agencies back to the families themselves.

Two federal laws have affected the development of family preservation programs. In 1974, Public Law 93–45, the Juvenile Justice and Delinquency Prevention Act, encouraged states to deinstitutionalize status offenders. Public Law 96–272, the Adoption Assistance and Child Welfare Act, which came into effect in October, 1982, mandates states to make reasonable efforts to maintain children in their own homes before making out-of-home placements. It encourages states to reconsider their policies and work toward preserving and reunifying families. Some states have clearly voiced their support for family preservation programs. States such as California, Colorado, New York, Ohio, and Washington have passed legislation encouraging the initiation of family preservation programs. Other states, like Oregon and

New Hampshire, have not passed state legislation but have made policy decisions, reallocating funding to support such programs. It is useful to consider the ways in which state systems have either inhibited or encouraged these programs.

Although the federal government, through legal mandates, has endorsed and encouraged family preservation in a piecemeal fashion, most states do not consider this a priority. Out-of-home placement continues to be used readily, with little thought given to other alternatives. Both administrators and human service workers need to be educated about the efficacy of home-based family services. No matter how much federal and private money is spent on family preservation programs, the effort is futile unless endorsement of and commitment to this alternative occur at the state level. The federal government can initiate demonstration projects, and foundations and corporations can provide funding to develop family preservation programs, but states must eventually pick up the funding. By redirecting their funding from foster care, residential placement, and institutional care, states can support the more effective and more economical home-based family services.[7] Family counseling programs are also preventive. Altering family interaction patterns makes it less likely that other children in the family will exhibit dysfunctional behavior.[8]

Our main problem is not our lack of knowledge about how to help families; it is the need for commitment to the provision of high-quality family services. We must recognize, however, that family-centered services are not a panacea. It is necessary to create a balanced service delivery system, in which family preservation programs and out-of-home placement resources are seen as complementary, not adversarial.

This book is not intended to impart an understanding of federal and state policies on the implementation of family preservation programs; other books provide this information. However, discussion of family preservation programs must be considered within the context of the political arena. A political commitment to family preservation must be made on both the national and state levels. Foster care must be reconceptualized, and used as a family preservation service instead of a form of long-term placement.

This book presents a compilation of the available descriptive and programmatic material on the multiproblem family. Based on a review of the literature and the programs that have worked with this population in the past and the present, a comprehensive model is recommended. The need to develop such a comprehensive model becomes clear when the impact of multiproblem families on society is recognized.

Research first focused on the multiproblem family during the 1950s. After World War II, economic growth brought into focus a group of people who had failed to profit from the strong economy. Several studies indicated that a small group of families in each community examined was persistently troubled by many severe problems.[9] The most well-known study was in November, 1948, in St. Paul, Minnesota; it revealed that only 6 percent of families used over half of the city's social services. These families had serious problems, such as ill-health, maladjustment, and dependency. Most had more than one problem.[10] "Many agencies had been working concurrently with these families over an extended period of time but . . . treatment had been fragmentary, episodic, individually oriented, and on an agency-by-agency basis, according to the particular symptom that was causing trouble either to the family or the community at the time."[11] Hence, the impact of multi-problem families on society and on social service agencies is disproportionate to the total number of families.

A little-known, five-year study, initiated in 1962 by the Massachusetts Committee of Children and Youth, substantiates the results of the St. Paul project. This study contrasted two areas of Massachusetts — the Central Berkshire area and the city of Somerville — in an effort to find ways to increase the effectiveness of state programs for children and their families and to improve service provision. The study found that there was little co-ordination of services among state agencies; that services were fragmented, with each agency providing specialized, not comprehensive, services; and that multiproblem families used services far out of proportion to their total numbers. As a result of the study, it was recommended that service provision be comprehensive since "it is illogical to assume that one set of problems and needs is completely isolated from all the other problems and needs of the people in an area or community. In fact, they are all interrelated, and so a broad comprehensive approach is needed."[12]

Working with Multiproblem Families

1
Defining the Multiproblem Family

The term "multiproblem" needs to be clearly defined, as it is often misunderstood. Multiproblem families differ in size, structure, geographic location, presenting problem, and agency involvement. Most share the characteristics outlined in the following sections.

Characteristics of Multiproblem Families

More Than One Problem

The multiproblem family has a number of problems that cut across many dimensions of family life. Such a family can neither handle these problems itself nor find help in services available in the community. Its inability to cope with its problems distinguishes this family from others.

The multiproblem family is referred to social service agencies because of a symptom in one family member; however, more than one person needs help. The symptom does not indicate the magnitude of the real problem, but is only a sign that the family suffers from many problems that family members have failed to deal with for a long time.

Internal and External Problems

The multiproblem family is characterized by both internal (within the family) and external (between the family and community) problems. Both problem types must be considered in assessment and treatment.

Internal or Intrasystemic Problems. The multiproblem family is often referred to as disorganized. Aponte has created a more positive term to characterize this type of family. He considers it underorganized, suggesting "not so much an improper kind of organization, as a deficiency in the degree of constancy, differentiation, and flexibility of the structural organization of the family system."[1] Despite its chaos, the multiproblem family is organized, but in a dysfunctional fashion.

The family can be conceived of as a system, with some level of organization, in which members play roles that are reciprocal and complementary to the goals of the family. To ensure integration, the roles of family members must be directed toward the same goal. In underorganized families, roles are not integrated and the family is unable to work together to promote healthy system maintenance.[2]

Members of multiproblem families do not relate to each other in a healthy manner; instead, their behavior often frustrates attempts to unite the family. A dysfunctional pattern in family relationships is reinforced in each attempt to resolve problems. Repeated negative interactions destroy the possibility of positive communication and understanding among family members.

External or Intersystemic Problems. The multiproblem family is also characterized by external problems. These may be economic, educational, or vocational. Such external problems may include the family's inability to get help from community agencies because it does not know how to access services or because it has been thoroughly overwhelmed by the service system and/or angered by past encounters because of the failure of human service agencies to meet the family's needs.

Multiproblem families are often isolated and alienated, possessing few, if any, positive support networks. Most face many day-to-day environmental stresses, such as high crime, drugs, poor housing, health problems, and financial difficulties. The income of many of these families is near or below poverty level. In many cases, they are struggling to "stay alive"; meeting basic needs is the priority.

Because of the psychological and financial burdens of poverty, children of poor families are in more danger of being placed in foster care. Since minority children are disproportionately poor, they are "especially vulnerable to inappropriate placements and inadequate care. Often, they are over-represented in child care systems, and they may receive differential treatment."[3]

Too often, a family's problems are viewed as a pathology endemic to that family; the environment of the multiproblem family is often neglected in assessment and treatment. Many social workers would rather address intrapsychic and interpersonal problems than consider external problems that demand immediate attention. Treatment is sure to fail unless each family is considered within its environment, with a focus on problems that pose an immediate threat to family survival, such as lack of housing, employment, and food.

Chronicity and Crisis

Another characteristic of the multiproblem family is chronicity—family members have been failing for quite a while. The family's repeated appeals for help without following through, apathy toward services offered, or demanding attitude with little desire to discuss family problems have alienated social service agencies. Consequently, families often accuse agencies of being unable to help them. In addition to having numerous problems, the family's attitude toward and manner of dealing with its dilemmas demonstrate that it is unwilling to confront and improve its adverse conditions.

The multiproblem family is known for its frequent crises, which it consistently meets by breaking down. Typically the multiproblem family requests assistance when a crisis occurs, and then ceases contact with an agency until there is another crisis. Services respond to a specific symptom of one family member; the focus is not on the family as a whole. There is no provision for a continuing relationship between the agency and the family; only the crisis is addressed.

Multiproblem Agencies: Systems Interfacing with Families at Risk

Agencies label families as multiproblem and perceive them as disinterested in helping themselves. Most agencies do not understand these families, and traditional services fail to respond to their complex needs. Based on their histories of negative interactions with the social service system, multiproblem families feel angry, taken advantage of, and misunderstood. This attitude is realistic considering the families' experiences; agencies have not only been unhelpful, they have often worsened situations. A family's instinct is to survive: to protect itself from further dealings with agencies.

Often the service systems involved with a multiproblem family work in isolation, providing fragmented and duplicated services that are unplanned and crisis-oriented. "Services tend to have grown up piecemeal and not in response to a well co-ordinated plan. They have been designed predominantly for the individual rather than the family, and each service tends to have responsibility for one particular symptom of disorganization."[4]

From the family's point of view, social workers exacerbate family crises. Uncoordinated, individual-focused service creates more difficulty for the family than it already has.[5] Such service also reflects the family's disorganized way of handling its problems. The family's initial anger at itself for being unable to resolve its problems is then focused on social workers, who have not only been unable to help but have recreated the family's confusion. Considering a family's distrust of social workers, it is ludicrous to expect it to relate to a number of workers at a time. A more logical approach is to encourage the family to establish a trusting relationship with one worker or team, with the eventual goal of interfacing with other workers.

Families at risk are identified through the school, health, social service, mental health, and criminal justice systems. Frequently more than one family member is determined to be at risk by one of these systems, and it is not unusual for these systems to deal with more than one generation of a family.

An example of the numerous systems interfacing with a multiproblem family can be seen in the Conan family, whose case illustrates the provision of uncoordinated, individual-focused treatment. Jim, the identified client, is sixteen years old and has been adjudicated delinquent. He is also an alcohol and drug abuser and receives counseling and medical treatment for substance abuse from the community mental health center while he continues to live at home. He regularly attends Alcoholics Anonymous and Narcotics Anonymous meetings. Jim's mother is an alcoholic who recently became seriously ill and was diagnosed as having cancer. Mrs. Conan receives medical attention and counseling from a social worker at the local hospital. Her husband, who is involved in criminal activities, is in and out of jail. Thus, the boy deals with the health, mental health, and criminal justice systems; his mother interfaces with the health and mental health systems; his father is involved in the criminal justice system.

Significance of the System That Identifies a Client

The system that identifies a client determines treatment. This is portrayed by the services available to a seventeen-year-old drug abuser. If this youth is referred to an agency specializing in drug treatment, counseling focuses specifically on drug abuse, with little discussion of other problems and no consideration of the youth within his or her environment. In fact, in some states, private agencies funded by the state are instructed to focus only on their clients' drug involvement to the exclusion of all else. If this youth is referred to a mental health clinic, his or her drug problem is viewed as a symptom of emotional problems and psychotherapy is provided. If the youth is referred to a family service agency, family systems treatment is employed. Although simplistic, this example illustrates the importance of the system that identifies a client.

A few years ago, the state of Maine developed five family preservation programs with different "trigger" or referral mechanisms. Youths were referred to two of the programs by the juvenile justice system; in a third program, youths were referred by protective services; in a fourth program, youths were referred for substance abuse; and in a fifth program, youths were referred because of suspension from or dropping out of school. Edward Hinckley, Director of Children's Services for Maine's Department of Mental Health and Mental Retardation, points out that "it doesn't matter who identifies the problem or what label you put on it, it's the same kid, same problem, same type of family dysfunction and fortunately the same kinds of interventions seem to be effective." This experiment shows that a service system need not determine a client's treatment according to the system's area of specialization. Placing a label on a client fails to address his or her needs.

It is unfortunate that the system that identifies a client so greatly determines the treatment.

Familiarity with the Social Service System

The multiproblem family is too familiar with the social service system. It is a client of several agencies and has often been referred to as a "multiagency" family. It is not uncommon for a family to return to an agency year after year, requesting assistance for a recurring problem. For example, Mrs. Brown, with her four children, approaches a local human service agency, seeking housing. She claims her husband beats her and she desperately wants to move out. The agency encourages her to take out a restraining order and agrees to help her find housing, but Mrs. Brown decides to return to her husband. A year later, Mrs. Brown returns to the same agency, again bringing her children along. She reiterates the problem that brought her in a year earlier. For the second time, Mrs. Brown refuses to take out a restraining order and again she chooses to return home.

The problems of multiproblem families are generational. Unless intervention is provided, the children of multiproblem families are very likely to have problems similar to those of their parents. For example, a mother who had truancy problems and dropped out of high school when she was a youth may have children who follow in her footsteps.

The Process of Mutual Withdrawal

Social workers characterize the multiproblem family as hard-core, deprived, distrustful, unmotivated, hopeless, and difficult, if not impossible, to reach. The family's relationship with social service agencies is negative, and the agencies describe the attitude of the family as ranging from indifferent to hostile. Agencies slowly withdraw their services from the multiproblem family because the family fails to exhibit appropriate behavior and live up to the standards of society and the expectations of the agencies. The relationship between human service agencies and the multiproblem family is characterized by mutual alienation.

The multiproblem family experiences the stigma of being known and disliked by many human service agencies. This family has failed repeatedly, and despite the reasons for its failure, the outcome remains tantamount and consistent: the multiproblem family has been unable to achieve what society considers success.

There is also mutual withdrawal between the multiproblem family and society. When a family is failing and feels rejected and ostracized, it withdraws by behaving in a manner that is unacceptable to society. It is then rejected again, and the cycle continues. Society and its institutions withdraw from the multiproblem family, not only because it is failing, but also because it appears to be unresponsive to help. When society labels a family as unreachable and impossible and withdraws its involvement, chronicity is the tragic result.

Like the institutions representing society, the family also withdraws. It is frustrated by its many failures and its negative experiences with the social service system. This mutual rejection and withdrawal grows extreme as the gap between family and community widens.

Based on past encounters, the multiproblem family has negative expectations of the social service system. Given a stigma and labeled by institutions in the community, it is not surprising that the family is antagonistic when approached by the "helping" profession. "The feeling that innumerable forces are impinging on one's life without an ability to determine the type or quantity or impact of such forces is very disorganizing to either family, individual personality, or both."[7]

The initial step in working with such a family is to decrease the mutual withdrawal between the family and society. Inevitably, the family will believe that social workers are rejecting and unaccepting. The family's attitude of "here we go again" is based on reality. Having failed repeatedly and having been involved with numerous agencies, the family's hostility toward interacting with a system in which it feels rejected, alienated, and incompetent is not unfounded. Similarly, the frustration and lack of interest of social service agencies toward the multiproblem family is also understandable.

2

Working from Health, Not Pathology

A family generates a good deal of information. What information is considered important depends upon the conceptual framework employed. Too often a counselor is unaware of the perspective within which the family system is assessed. Two basic models are used to assess family problems.

The Growth Development Model versus the Medical Model

The medical model is the most traditional of the models. A counselor using this model diagnoses a family as having a certain degree of "sickness" or pathology. The family is immediately perceived in a negative or pathological light. The growth development model, however, views the family as stuck in a rigid pattern that it does not know how to change. This model assumes that change is possible. The counselor recognizes that the family is doing the best it can. "Within their particular way of seeing the world, their behavior usually seems like the only or best option available to them at that particular moment."[1]

The medical model implies a static, rigid perception of reality. This model assumes that a certain percentage of the population is healthy, a certain percentage is normal, and a certain percentage is pathological. A person is either healthy, normal, or pathological, and the therapist defines the category in which an individual fits. The medical model is pathologically based, with the goal of determining who is "sick," why they are "sick," and how their "sickness" can be controlled.

The growth development model assumes that everyone begins at the same point and that each person has potential. This model is not based on the belief that the population is divided into healthy, normal, and pathological types. Instead, it considers that personal development is fluid and characterized by constant movement or growth, with ups and downs. The growth development model provides a framework with which to assess where people are in their development, with the goal of helping them move to the next developmental stage.

The medical model focuses on family weaknesses, whereas the growth development model emphasizes family strengths. The latter is more beneficial because it diagnoses a family within a positive framework; it initiates contact with a family by perceiving it in a potentially healthy framework. The growth development model employs an educational rather than a therapeutic approach. Instead of categorizing the family as "sick," it is characterized as lacking skills.

Conceptualizing a family as potentially healthy, rather than from a problem-oriented perspective, sets the stage for a more positive relationship between counselor and family. This approach also increases a family's receptivity to a counselor's interventions. In addition, this approach considers that at least maintaining its present level of functioning is a success for the family, and conveys this feeling to family members, giving them hope that their situation can improve. The manner in which a counselor initially approaches a family determines whether or not a trusting relationship ensues.

The growth development model assumes that the goal of treatment is to facilitate client growth. The counselor conveys concern and respect for the family, accepts family members as they are, and begins with what they perceive as their most pressing problems. Finding ways to help resolve problems in partnership with the family is the counselor's goal. One of the counselor's primary emphases is to encourage families to use support resources (such as other family members, public agencies, and self-help groups), which these families often are unaware of, overlook, or are hesitant to use.

Mrs. Larch is a forty-nine-year-old recovering alcoholic. She is married, has seven children, and lives in the city. When the Larch family became involved in a family counseling program, the counselor learned that Mrs. Larch was an expert at rug hooking. Mrs. Larch taught the family counselor how to hook a rug, and eventually other mothers in the program expressed an interest in learning. A weekly mothers' group evolved. At first, group members were taught rug hooking by Mrs. Larch. As time went on, however, other mothers shared their expertise with the group, and members discussed their husbands, children, and jobs. In addition, group members went bowling, shopping, and to the movies together. Mrs. Larch received a good deal of recognition for her expertise in rug hooking from both the family counselor and group members. Her self-image improved as she recognized that she was a valuable person, able to help others. Soon Mrs. Larch began selling the items she had made, and this further enhanced her self-image.

This example illustrates how a family counselor encouraged the mother of a multiproblem family to develop her talents. Using the growth development model as a framework, the counselor conveyed a genuine respect for Mrs. Larch and accentuated her strengths rather than dwelling on her problems. This process enabled Mrs. Larch to develop a feeling of self-worth while finding strength to address problems in her life.

Dimensions of Healthy Family Functioning

A healthy family is one in which instrumental needs (such as housing, utilities, and food) and emotional needs are met. The family's relationship to the community is cooperative and productive, or at least neutral. If parents fail to meet the instrumental and emotional needs of their children, and relationships with the community are consistently negative, the family becomes dysfunctional.[2]

All too often, family counselors do not understand how a healthy family functions. Far too little research has been conducted in this area, whereas there is an abundance of research on the dysfunctional family.[3] Most human service workers are familiar with theories and treatment methods applied to dysfunctional families. Knowledge and understanding of how a healthy family functions enhance a counselor's ability to assess and treat problematic families and provide a framework of health from which to work.

A good deal of material is available on the stages of individual development in the human life cycle; however, the stages of the family life cycle have been considered only recently. An understanding of the normal development of both individuals and families provides a framework for treating dysfunctional families.

Barnhill conducted a thorough review of the processes comprising healthy family functioning. In his article, "Healthy Family Systems," Barnhill distinguishes eight dimensions of family health, which fall into four categories:

"I. Identity Processes
  1. Individuation vs isolation [should be "enmeshment"]
  2. Mutuality vs isolation

II. Change
  3. Flexibility vs rigidity
  4. Stability vs disorganization

III. Information Processing
  5. Clear vs unclear or distorted perception
  6. Clear vs unclear or distorted communication

IV. Role Structuring
  7. Role reciprocity vs unclear roles or role conflict
  8. Clear vs diffuse or breached generational boundaries."[4]

Although Barnhill uses "vs" to discuss concepts, it is important to realize that the processes characterizing family functioning occur on a continuum, not as polarities. A family system is always in motion and always changing. Whether or not family members are at the "right" place in terms of being healthy is very much related to where members are in their life cycles. For example, in discussing individuation versus enmeshment, it is appropriate for a six-month-old baby to be enmeshed with its mother; however, it is inappropriate for a teenager. A counselor attains an understanding of a family system by determining the developmental stage of each family member and by considering the issues relevant to that stage. The developmental stages of individual family members are considered within the context of the family's developmental stages. A healthy family will not necessarily remain healthy; it depends on how the family moves through each developmental stage.

Identity Processes

Individuation concerns the ability of each family member to be autonomous. It is characterized by a sense of independence, identity, and clear personal boundaries. Satir describes the individuated person as having "faith in his own competence. He is able to ask others for help, but he believes he can make his own decisions and is his own best resource."[5]

Individuation is illustrated in the following case example of a single-parent family. Mrs. Barth has trouble accepting her daughter Robin as an adolescent who is struggling with her own identity and needs. This difficulty causes numerous fights and clashes between Robin and her mother. Mrs. Barth cannot understand why her daughter needs privacy. Robin does not want to go shopping with her mother; instead, she prefers to be with her friends. She also declines when asked to join her mother for a movie. Consequently, mother and daughter grow apart and hardly communicate. Both need to learn to accept each other and at the same time meet each other's needs. Once Mrs. Barth can let go of and accept her daughter, Robin is more apt to accommodate her mother at times when she knows her mother needs her. A counselor helps the family create more flexible boundaries, so that each member has space to grow.

Enmeshment is characterized by unclear personal boundaries and an identity that is determined by others. The enmeshed person is overinvolved with others. "The greatest danger, that of losing one's own self, may pass off quietly as if it were nothing; every other loss, that of an arm, a leg, five dollars, a wife, etc., is sure to be noticed."[6]

Enmeshment is described in the following case example. Mrs. Michaels is separated from her husband and is the mother of four children. She came to the United States from Greece and still personifies the family tradition, which she has faithfully instilled in her children. Mrs. Michaels considers the family as a unified entity, comprised of individuals whose first priority is the family. Respect for the elderly, attending family functions, making oneself available when needed, are sine qua non in this family. Any attempt by a family member to separate is hampered by Mrs. Michaels, and viewed as a betrayal. The Michaels represent an enmeshed family, in which Mrs. Michaels is overinvolved with family members.

Mutuality can only occur between individuals who possess a clear sense of themselves. Isolation, on the other hand, is characterized by a feeling of estrangement. This feeling develops in one of two situations: when a family member feels uninvolved and isolated from the family or when family members are so enmeshed and overinvolved that they are isolated from their own identities. Developing individuation and mutuality is essential to overcome overinvolvement or estrangement.

Change

Flexibility is the ability to respond and adjust to different situations. Rigidity is resistance and an inability to adapt to change, as illustrated by consistently repetitious and redundant responses. Stability involves finding predictability and safety in family interchanges. In a stable family, an open expression of feelings and thoughts is encouraged, and disagreement does not limit future interactions or threaten the family with disintegration. Disorganization, on the other hand, reflects a lack of security and consistency within the family. Flexibility and stability characterize the healthy family—in contrast to rigid, redundant responses, refusal to adapt to changing situations, or "underorganized" responses that inhibit stability.

Information Processing

Clear perception entails a realistic understanding of oneself and others. Clear communication involves direct interchanges among family members. Unclear perceptions are uncertain, ambiguous, or conflictual; they result from indirect communication. Without clear perceptions and clear communication, information cannot be realistically processed. Assessing the manner in which family members process information is essential in determining family health.

Role Structuring

Role reciprocity concerns mutually complementary behavior, in which an individual's role is compatible with his or her partner's. Uncomplementary behavioral patterns in a family lead to unclear roles, role conflict, and continuing problems. Clear generational boundaries are those in which lines of authority are understood and boundaries between generations are clearly delineated. A diffuse generational boundary is dysfunctional, and involves a member of one generation who is more closely allied with another generation than with his or her own generation—for example, a strong parent-child alliance. A breached generational boundary is dysfunctional as well, and entails an alliance between individuals from two generations against another person—for example, mother and child against father.

    The eight dimensions of healthy family functioning described above are interconnected; thus, healthy processes within a family are reciprocal. Improvement in a family system can begin with any dimension and will generalize, strengthening the functioning of other dimensions. The following cases show the contrast between a functional family and a multiproblem family with similar problems.

Family Systems in a Multiproblem and a Functional Family

The Multiproblem Family

Mrs. Epson is a single parent, with seven children. She and five of her children live in the city. Mrs. Epson's oldest son, Bob, thirty-two years of age, was committed to the juvenile justice system as a youth, and is currently in prison for armed robbery. Her daughter, Karen, twenty-one, was also committed to the juvenile justice system. To avoid being placed in a residential facility, Karen got married, had a child, and then got divorced. She lived with a boyfriend, had another child, and decided to end this relationship. Shortly after Karen moved into an apartment with her two children, her first husband beat her badly and she became a paraplegic. Karen's children were temporarily placed in foster care by the state because she was unable to care for them. Darren, Mrs. Epson's twenty-year-old son, was also committed to the juvenile justice system and is currently in prison for murder. Like his older siblings, Tim, seventeen, is committed to the juvenile justice system. For two years he was in a family counseling program, and did very well until his involvement with the program ended. Then he resumed his involvement with drugs, and appeared in court for possession and sale of marijuana. Janet, age sixteen, is obese, like her mother. She has always had difficulty in school and has a poor self-image. Janet recently had a baby. Sue, age fourteen, became pregnant a few months after Janet. Mary, the youngest child, age nine, was in foster care for two years, but is currently living with her mother. Karen, Tim, Janet, Sue, and Mary live with their mother, as do Karen's and Janet's children. Mrs. Epson's husband lives with the family on and off, and is involved in criminal activities. Mrs. Epson spends most of her time watching television in bed. She is an alcoholic and also regularly uses tranquilizers and marijuana. She is too overwhelmed by her children's problems to find a way to help them. If anything, Mrs. Epson encourages their criminal activities by allowing them to bring stolen goods into the house.

The Functional Family

Mrs. Slater is divorced and lives with her boyfriend in a housing project in a suburban community. She works part time as a waitress and collects welfare. She has five children, four of whom live with her. Her oldest son, John, is twenty and lives with his girlfriend. Her second oldest boy, Bob, eighteen, is graduating from high school. Her third son, Richard, is sixteen years old, and is committed to the juvenile justice system for stealing. He recently quit school and refuses to find a job. Although he is lazy and watches television all day, Mrs. Slater is determined to help him. Her youngest boy, Mike, age thirteen, is regularly truant from school. Joanne, age nine, is the youngest child and exhibits no problems.

Truancy was a problem for Mrs. Slater when she was in high school. Although it is an issue for each of her children (except the youngest child), the two oldest managed to graduate from high school. Mrs. Slater is committed to helping her children and is available when they need her. She makes a habit of addressing problems as they arise. Mrs. Slater and her boyfriend have a positive relationship. Although they have their differences, their love for each other is apparent to the children. Despite their problems, family members are warm and caring. They love and support each other, and manage to stick together.

Summary

Although both families have problems, the functional family is able to cope. There is positive communication among family members and a feeling of caring is prevalent. The family works together to resolve its problems, and asserts family solidarity. In the multiproblem family, there is little or no positive connection among family members; each individual is isolated and alone. The parental subsystem is weak and often nonexistent because Mrs. Epson is involved in alcohol and drugs and her husband is seldom home.

Systems Theory and Terminology

Understanding systems theory and its terminology is useful in assessment and treatment, and helps a family worker understand the structures and processes that characterize the multiproblem family.[1] In his book, *Families and Family Therapy,* Minuchin explains structural family therapy, and describes systems terminology. This book is mandatory reading for those working with families. A brief overview of the key concepts in structural family therapy is given in the following sections.

Systems

The family is a system composed of people and their communication. When two individuals interact, their communication defines their relationship. A system can be compared to a tuning fork; when you strike one end, the other end reverberates—a person cannot *not* communicate.

Patterns

All therapy is based on the identification of patterns, which are redundant, recurring interactions. A counselor determines the patterns within the family; patterns can be either rigid or flexible. Rigid patterns are dysfunctional. An individual with a rigid pattern has few responses available. For example, a rigid pattern is apparent if each time a counselor asks the wife a question, she looks at her husband before answering. In such a case, the wife is unable to maintain her autonomy. A flexible pattern is healthy, and is shown by an individual who has many responses available and who can adapt to a variety of situations. For example, if a boy asks his mother whether he can go to the movies, and his mother sometimes says "yes" and sometimes "no," in response to the situation, she has a flexible pattern. If a mother tells her son he cannot go to the movies each time he asks, she shows a rigid pattern.

Rules

Each pattern is composed of rules or injunctions about behavior that have consequences. Rules indicate the norms of a family. When a counselor recognizes a family's patterns, he or she can infer the rules. Rules are implicit and unwritten; indirectly expressed and inferred; reoccurring over time; self-perpetuating; and a parsimonious way of dealing with a lot of data. Rules take on the coloration or style of their system, and there are rules about how to make rules.[2] The guidelines that govern the limits of individual expression within the family are its rules. For example, a youth can stay out late once, but if he stays out late three times, he has gone too far. Rules

3

The Family System as the Primary Unit of Treatment

Counselors often diagnose and treat each family member with little regard for the interrelationships within the family system. A counselor may initially find it difficult to view the family as an interlocking web of relationships, particularly if trained in individual counseling. But perceiving the family as a unit is most effective for assessment and treatment. This is not to say, however, that an individual within a family does not have personal problems that require attention.

Focusing on the Family

In working with a family, the counselor repeatedly conveys that he or she perceives the family as a unit. This approach takes the focus away from the identified client, and makes the family aware that they need to work together to resolve problems. Typically, a family comes to a counselor expecting that he or she will "fix" the person the family has identified as the "problem." Family members expect to have minimal involvement in the process. The family worker must assist family members in recognizing that a family system is composed of a number of interlocking relationships, some positive and some negative; that family members contribute to the maintenance of the identified client's symptom; and that a family must agree to work together, as a unit, to change their situation.

The following case example indicates the impact of family members on each other. The Hecker family is referred to a social service agency when Bill, fifteen, becomes involved with the juvenile court. Initially, a family worker meets with Mrs. Hecker, while Bill is seen by a counselor. After a few individual meetings with Bill, the counselor learns that Bill has a drinking problem and recommends a family session involving all the members. The meeting enables the family members to express their feelings about Bill's drinking and how it affects them. Bill, who has no idea of the effect his drinking has had on his family, is taken aback, and for the first time is willing to acknowledge his drinking problem.

must be age-appropriate. Many parents set rules and do not realize that they must change them as their children grow older. Parents need to be flexible and understand child development.

The following example illustrates a rule that is understood by all family members. Within the Jackson family, everyone knows that one should not talk while someone else is talking. Although unspoken, this rule is understood by each family member. It remains with the family over time, is self-perpetuating, and is learned by watching other family members. Typically, family members bring rules they have learned in their own families into their marriages. The fact that there are rules about how to make rules is illustrated by a mother deciding that her daughter will take out the garbage once a week. This rule tells you that mother has the power to make rules in the family. Two rules, not one, are evident.

A rule is fixed when an abstraction influences an individual's behavior as if the abstraction were concrete. For example, if a family is categorized as violent by a human service agency, whether the family is truly violent is irrelevant, since the human service agency has labeled it violent and treats it as such. The rule that this is a violent family has been reified. Similarly, if a father continually tells his son that he is stupid and treats him as such, the father reifies the rule—it becomes a reality.

Structure

Family structure is determined by who interacts with whom and under what conditions. Patterns determine family structure. For example, the structure of a family is indicated by a father who only talks to his daughter through the mother. Mother is a go-between for father and daughter.

Subsystems

Family structure is determined by subsystems within the family, which allow for differentiation of tasks and encourage autonomous exploration and mastery. Subsystems are defined by age, gender, and interest. Each family has many subsystems; a husband and wife compose one subsystem, and children make up another. If a father and his son both like to ride motorcycles, they are bound together by their common interest and compose a subsystem.

When examining families, the counselor delineates, for both him or herself and the family, the subsystems of husband and wife and of mother and father. Often a family worker fails to distinguish between these two subsystems. How mother and father relate to their children is different from the way they relate as husband and wife. During family meetings, the counselor outlines the dual roles of husband and wife and of mother and father.

Boundaries

Boundaries are rules that determine the limits of a subsystem. There are three types of boundaries: enmeshed or overinvolved, clear or balanced, and disengaged or underinvolved.[3] The definition of enmeshment is that boundaries are constantly violated. They are undifferentiated and have too much information passing through. For example, every time a youngster tries to do her math homework, her mother tells her that like her mother, she will never be able to master math. Mother is confusing her identity with her daughter's identity. If the daughter believes her mother, the enmeshment becomes pathological and the daughter takes on that aspect of her mother's personality. Although this is one minute example of enmeshment, it should be noted that enmeshment may be the beginning of severe emotional disturbance. Another example of enmeshment is illustrated by a family in which no one is permitted to close the doors to their rooms. There is neither privacy nor permission to be alone; boundaries are enmeshed.

A clear or balanced boundary is one that permits just enough information to be exchanged among family members. Members are close, yet autonomous. The Cox family exemplifies a healthy family, in which individuation and autonomy are encouraged and reinforced. Boundaries within this family are clear. Both Mr. and Mrs. Cox encourage their children to freely express themselves. As parents, they try to be nonjudgmental and understanding. There are clear limits, and everyone knows the rules by which they are expected to abide. Family outings and activities involve everyone, not only in the activities themselves, but also in the decision making and the preparations. If appropriate, the problem of one family member is discussed openly by all the members, who hope to help the person resolve his or her problem. Sometimes families form subgroupings, in which two or more family members group together to deal with a problem without involving all the family members.

With a disengaged boundary, not enough information is exchanged. Disengagement is often signaled by neglect. The following case example illustrates disengagement. Mrs. Starr, her daughter Linda, age thirteen, and Mrs. Starr's mother share an apartment. Mrs. Starr works for the telephone company. Most of the day, she is busy at her job and is unaware of Linda's whereabouts and activities. When Mrs. Starr is home, Linda refuses to talk to her mother. Linda is free to come and go, and her mother expresses little interest or concern. Mrs. Starr also goes about her activities without informing either her mother or daughter of her whereabouts. Consequently, these three individuals lead separate lives, even though they share the same living space and at times eat their meals together.

Boundaries range along a continuum between extremes. Family boundaries shift according to circumstances. For example, after a death, a family may be more enmeshed or more disengaged, depending how the family handles the stresses of a death. Flexibility in responding to specific situations is necessary. If the family unit or individual members are unable to adjust their boundaries to reality, they become "stuck" and respond in a rigid manner. When determining a family's potential to interact in a flexible, healthy manner, the counselor assesses the boundaries that characterize and indicate family structure.

Detouring

Detouring within the family occurs when stress originating in one subsystem crosses the boundary into another subsystem. When stress somewhere in the family system is too difficult to handle, it surfaces elsewhere in the system. Detouring is a major concept in family therapy. For example, a husband tells his wife that she is a sloppy housekeeper and the wife changes the subject and talks about their child's misbehavior in school. Stress in the husband-wife subsystem is inappropriately transferred across the boundary to the child subsystem. Another example of detouring is exemplified by a wife who, after a hard day at work, comes home and yells at her husband, who in turn becomes upset and yells at his son and daughter. Recognizing detouring within a family system is important; it may be the major way in which husband and wife relate.

Restructuring

Working cooperatively, the counselor and the family restructure dysfunctional family patterns to alleviate family problems. For example, if mother and daughter are enmeshed, and the daughter repeatedly looks at her mother when the counselor asks her questions, the counselor can restructure the situation by sitting between daughter and mother. The mother is seated next to the father, clearly marking family boundaries and encouraging daughter's autonomy. Another example of restructuring is when a wife accuses her husband of not taking any responsibility for their children and he changes the subject, focusing on their daughter's shoplifting. The counselor can bring the focus back to the spouse subsystem, thus "freeing" the child.

It is essential for family workers to understand the systems theory and terminology outlined in the preceding sections. This knowledge enables counselors to determine whether family counseling is appropriate for a particular family, and guides them in how to intervene to improve family functioning.

4
Developing an Intake System

Establishing specific criteria for referral insures that referral sources recognize which families would be best helped by family counseling. It is useful to hold workshops that highlight the types of families that benefit from family counseling and describe the program's assessment and treatment approaches. Often referring workers are unfamiliar with a family systems approach. Providing an overview of the program obviates unrealistic expectations about whom it serves and what it can accomplish.

Criteria for Referral: Family Types

A number of family types seem more likely to benefit from family counseling than others. A useful but noninclusive list, categorized by family systems, not symptoms, is presented in the following sections.

Families with Chronic Boundary Problems

In families with boundary problems, enmeshment or disengagement is evident, and the problems are longstanding. Parent and child subsystems have unclear boundaries. The following example illustrates a family with chronic boundary problems. Mr. and Mrs. Hopedale have three children, thirteen, sixteen, and seventeen. They have always been very involved with their children. Their oldest daughter recently ran away from home, and within the same week, her sixteen-year-old brother became involved with the juvenile court when he purchased alcohol as a minor. Both parents are alarmed at the situation and feel out of control.

When the family counselor intervenes, he learns that Mrs. Hopedale "lives for her children." She stays home each night in case anything happens. She frequently calls the children's friends to see if her children are where they say they will be. She left her part-time job at the fire station when her son went to court, so that she could devote more time to her family. Mrs. Hopedale is overinvolved or enmeshed with her children.

The family counselor helps Mrs. Hopedale give her children more autonomy by having the children show their mother that they can be trusted. Her children and her husband encourage Mrs. Hopedale to return to her job and to go out at night without worrying about the children. Mr. Hopedale takes on more responsibility for the children, thus relieving some of the burden previously placed upon his wife.

Families with a Parental Child

Another type of family that can benefit from family counseling is the family that allocates parental power to a child. This is a natural arrangement in large families, single-parent families, or families in which both parents work. The arrangement can be very functional and realistic, except when the parental child becomes stuck in this role and is not given flexibility to be a child.

The following case describes a family with a parental child. Before Mrs. Deer began attending Alcoholics Anonymous meetings, she often left the house for long periods of time. Diane, thirteen, assumed responsibility for her nine-year-old brother, Charles. Diane made sure Charles did his homework before he went out to play, prepared supper for both of them, and put Charles to bed by eight o'clock. Although Diane exhibited maturity in every aspect of her brother's care, she had problems caring for herself. Instead of attending school, Diane stayed at home, cleaning the house. Often she roamed the streets in search of her mother. Diane was stuck in the role of parental child. Her mother had abdicated the parental functions to her and did not allow her to be a child.

A family worker helps Mrs. Deer recognize that her daughter maintains the role of parental child in order to hold the family together. Mrs. Deer and the counselor discuss the adverse affects on Diane and talk about how to relieve Diane of her parental role. They consider ways to encourage Diane to participate in age-appropriate activities such as being with friends, attending school, and participating in recreational activities. The counselor supports Mrs. Deer's efforts to deal with her alcoholism and also encourages her to become involved in a parent support group.

Families in Transitional Situations

A family in a transitional situation is involved in divorce, marriage, death, moving, or has suffered a temporary loss or separation—for example, the father is in jail or the mother is in another state for a year. The following case describes a family in a transitional situation. When Mrs. Carol moved in with Mrs. Marsh and her two children, Peggy, fourteen, and Philip, eleven, there were traumatic repercussions. Mrs. Carol was more than a tenant; she and Mrs. Marsh were lovers. Their relationship was not openly acknowledged, but Peggy and Philip expressed their resentment and objection in many indirect ways. Peggy stopped attending school, joined a gang of boys who smoked pot, and engaged in petty crimes. Philip, previously an open and talkative youngster, became very quiet and withdrawn.

A family counselor helps Mrs. Marsh and Mrs. Carol recognize and understand the trauma Peggy and Philip experienced when Mrs. Carol moved in. The women's relationship is brought into the open through a meeting with all involved. In addition, Mrs. Marsh and the family counselor meet with the children to be sure they understand the situation between their mother and her lover, and to reiterate their mother's love and concern for the children. Every week, Mrs. Marsh spends time alone with each youngster to insure that her caring and interest are clearly conveyed.

Families in Which There Is Detouring

In families that detour an identified client exhibits a symptom. The client is, in effect, putting up a red flag, calling attention to a problem in the family. The identified client is not necessarily the real problem. It is the counselor's task to broaden the focus to include the entire family system.

In the case of the Marsh family, Peggy's truancy and delinquency are only symptoms of the actual problem. Peggy is unable to express her feelings about her mother's lover and cannot change the situation. In her frustration and helplessness she turns to negative behavior as a way to draw attention to herself and her family; Peggy is asking for help.

Families in Which Parents Have Unrealistic Expectations of Their Children

In families where parents expect too much of their children, the parents do not understand normal child development. They have little knowledge of the needs and behaviors appropriate for their child at each developmental stage. Some parents expect their youngsters to act like adults and to assume adult responsibilities. When children fail to meet their parents' unrealistic expectations, they are often punished. The counselor needs to educate the parents and help them attain realistic, age-appropriate expectations. The following case illustrates a parent's unrealistic expectations of her daughter. Jennifer Morton, the youngest of six children, is the only child still living with her mother. Mrs. Morton raised Jennifer alone and cannot accept the fact that her daughter, about to become sixteen, desperately needs to develop her own identity. Mrs. Morton refuses to let Jennifer go out with her friends, talk on the telephone, or go shopping with them. She expects her daughter to be with her at all times, and considers her a friend and peer. Furthermore, Mrs. Morton, who holds a full-time job, expects Jennifer to be responsible for all household chores.

The family worker discusses Jennifer's developmental needs with Mrs.

Morton. The worker asks Mrs. Morton to design a chart listing all the household chores. Chores are divided between mother and daughter, and time is allocated for Jennifer to spend with her friends. Jennifer receives an allowance for doing her chores and her resentment about having to do everything is alleviated. Designing a chart and allocating the chores between herself and her daughter build Mrs. Morton's competence and confidence in her ability to be a mother. The family worker focuses on guiding Mrs. Morton into a parental role, involving her in a parent support group, and helping her recognize the need for her daughter to become autonomous.

Underorganized Families

Underorganized families handle crises with great difficulty. Such families have no model for addressing crises and are unaware of community resources that can offer assistance. Mrs. Lynch is forty years old and has five children ranging from four to sixteen years of age. Her husband left her twelve years ago, and she has been living in a two-room apartment since then. She does not work and rarely has enough food for her children. Mrs. Lynch spends most of her time watching television and sleeping. She seldom leaves the house because she is embarrassed and overwhelmed by her obesity. The electricity went off a week ago and Mrs. Lynch does not have money to pay her bills. She is very concerned because it is October and is getting cold.

A family worker's first goal is to help Mrs. Lynch meet immediate needs, such as getting the electricity turned on and having enough food. The counselor advocates for Mrs. Lynch, and shows her how to obtain financial assistance. The counselor then focuses on building Mrs. Lynch's self-confidence; she is encouraged to get out of bed and get dressed each day. This is accomplished by setting small goals to insure success. The family worker meets Mrs. Lynch at 9:00 A.M., two days a week, to take her out for coffee and to go shopping. Over time, two days becomes four days, until Mrs. Lynch can mobilize herself daily. She is also encouraged to participate in a parent support group in an effort to build her self-esteem, provide a forum for her to talk with other parents, and foster friendships between Mrs. Lynch and her peers.

Determining Intake Processes and Procedures

Besides developing clear intake criteria, an agency must also devise specific intake processes and procedures. When creating an intake system, an agency clarifies—in writing—which family types are best served by family counseling, to whom families are referred, and what materials describing a family's history and prior treatment are required. The responsibilities of the referring agency and the family counseling agency are clearly delineated verbally, then in writing. Written clarification alleviates the possibility of misunderstanding and fosters a positive relationship between agencies. A flow chart showing intake procedures is useful.

The type of information a family counseling agency requests from the referring agency varies. Typically, agencies ask for more background data on families than they need. The following materials should be requested: a release of information form signed by the family; a list of agencies that have served the family in the past or are serving them at present; and a statement detailing the reasons for referral and the goals of the referring agency for the family.

Extensive assessments from agencies who previously worked with referred families are unnecessary. Family counselors often become overwhelmed by assessments of other service providers that describe a family as "impossible" or "hopeless." Such assessments create a negative framework from which to begin treatment. If the referring agency insists on sending assessments, the counselor must not consider them sacred. These assessments should be read after a counselor meets the family and forms his or her own impressions without preconceived notions.

When a family is referred to an agency, intake is conducted by the counselor assigned to work with the family. An intake form should be completed, containing the data needed to conduct family counseling and the information necessary to determine program efficacy. The form is not lengthy because multiproblem families have been to many agencies and are tired of answering the same questions. Formal assessments that entail elaborate testing delay treatment until the crisis has passed and the opportunity to make changes when motivation is high is lost. Intake is not a distinct stage that requires the family to provide large quantities of information at once; more information will be gathered during the early phase of treatment as or if it is needed.

Regular and frequent notes are kept on the progress of each family. Most referring agencies require a family counseling agency to submit reports on families. If no specific communication is mandated, the family counseling agency should submit a monthly progress report on each family. Counselors maintain frequent contact with referral sources, keeping them up to date and involved. This practice facilitates a positive relationship between agencies, and is especially useful when the referring agency assists in coordinating the treatment. For example, Bill and his family are referred to a family counseling program by the juvenile probation department. Bill meets his probation officer each week and also attends family meetings. The family counselor and probation officer maintain close contact and implement a coordinated treatment plan. During his meetings with Bill, the probation officer reinforces the family counselor's work with the family.

5
A Conceptual Framework for Assessment

Assessment continues throughout treatment. The more accurate the assessment, the better the treatment; if assessment is inaccurate, the subsequent treatment will be inappropriate. The initial assessment determines the type of intervention, and the conceptual framework from which an assessment is conducted greatly affects treatment. Assessment and treatment are inextricably connected.

Assessing Family Needs

During assessment, a family's strengths and weaknesses are evaluated on three levels:

Instrumental: each family member's ability or inability to negotiate the environment on his or her own behalf.

Intrapsychic: each family member's ability or inability to handle his or her emotions.

Interpersonal: each family member's ability or inability to handle interpersonal relationships.

The Instrumental Level

In assessing family strengths and weaknesses, the counselor gives priority to determining the family's ability to address concrete, everyday situations. Is the family able to utilize its environment to meet its needs? Is each family member succeeding in basic skill areas such as: hygiene, nutrition, medical and dental care, job, school, transportation, and recreation? Together with the family, the counselor determines if and how the family is surviving on a day-to-day basis and considers which areas require assistance.

Concrete needs are assessed before dealing with the deeper, more complex issues. By assisting in the resolution of instrumental needs, the counselor indicates to the family that he or she is interested in the concerns that family members consider most pressing and demonstrates that he or she can help. This is the best way to initiate a trusting relationship with a family who has never before received satisfaction from dealing with human service workers.

Family members learn to meet their basic needs by negotiating for community resources. If a mother is unable to pay her rent and has no job, how can she discuss intrapsychic or interpersonal problems? Her more immediate, pressing worries will take precedence.

The Intrapsychic Level

The second area of assessment is the intrapsychic level. How do family members handle emotions such as fear, joy, affection, depression, anxiety, and love? A family's strengths are recognized and weak intrapsychic skills are also determined. For example, if a father becomes upset, screams, and strikes his son, he needs to develop a positive way of handling his anger and disciplining his son. Is the father under stress in other areas of his life—for example, is he unemployed, having marital problems, or physically handicapped? Does the father treat his other children in the same way? These types of questions are explored.

A counselor analyzes the emotional climate of the family. Is affection expressed primarily by one person or is there a flexible give-and-take of affection within the family? If family members address the trouble they have in dealing with their emotions, they are better equipped to cope with everyday situations and their interpersonal relationships will improve.

The following case demonstrates the emotional climate of a family referred to a human service agency. Shouting is a common method of communication in the Norman family. Father yells and curses at mother; she in turn shouts at her children, and they yell back. Fighting, anger, hostility, and frustration ensue among all family members. When a family worker intervenes, it becomes obvious to family members that no one had been listening to the others; each had been preparing a rebuttal. Now, family members listen patiently to what each person is feeling as well as saying. Yelling is no longer necessary, since more effective patterns of communication have been learned.

The Interpersonal Level

The counselor assesses a family's ability to handle interpersonal situations and negotiate with others. Some areas assessed include: initiating contact with others, listening, meeting needs, negotiating in relationships, interacting with family members and peers, and interacting with authority figures.

The ability of an individual to handle interpersonal relationships is determined by his or her ability to manipulate the environment to meet his or her needs. Parents are role models, from whom their children learn patterns of interaction. The interpersonal skills that a child learns are the basis for how well the child is able to interact with others. A counselor assesses the communication skills of family members, and determines the interpersonal skills in which each is strong, as well as the skills that need improvement.

In the previous example, yelling was the customary pattern of behavior for the Norman children, Don and Hillary—not only at home, but also among their peers and in the classroom. Teachers complained bitterly about Don's shouting and cursing when he disagreed with others or was found at fault. Likewise, Hillary's teacher could not tolerate her attitude and conduct. When Mr. and Mrs. Norman altered their patterns of communication, their children were immediately affected and changed their communication styles. The children's teachers reported a positive change in both children.

Assessment Strategies

Broadening the Focus

Too often, agencies accept a family's definition of its problem: that the identified client is bad and needs help or should be removed from the home. Treating the identified client individually or taking the client from the home reinforces the family's definition; the identified client continues to be caught in a role assigned by the family. Family members are brought to counseling by the deviance or pain of the identified client, and the family expects that the counselor will change the identified client. The family wants the counselor to rectify the situation without affecting the family's ingrained patterns of interaction; that is, the family wants to change the results of its behavior without altering the behavior itself.

The counselor views the identified client as a family member who clearly indicates that a problem affects the entire family. The dysfunctional behavior exhibited by the identified client maintains the family system; this behavior insures a stable system. Instead of focusing on the identified client, the counselor's intervention treats the family as a unit. The counselor's task is to help the family conceptualize the problem from a family systems perspective.

Avoiding Blame

When assessing a family, a counselor supports and respects each family member. When defining goals, he or she speaks in terms of improving relationships in order to strengthen the functioning of the entire family system. The counselor does not blame a family member for a problem, because the counselor recognizes that more than one person contributes to a problem.

If a mother is unable to set firm limits, she is not at fault, because family members most likely contribute to her inability to establish and consistently enforce rules. For example, Mrs. Walker demands that Tricia be home no later than 7:30 P.M. Tricia, who wants to spend more time with her friends, never comes home before 10:00 P.M. Mr. Walker, unlike his wife, has no objection to his daughter coming home late. Mrs. Walker feels frustrated and stops trying to set limits for her daughter. She blames her failure to set limits on her husband's unwillingness to give her cooperation and support. With the aid of a family worker, the family makes some collective decisions that are accepted by everyone. Mrs. Walker is now able to set limits without anticipating objection and overrule.

Prioritizing Needs

Assessments determine the family's hierarchy of needs. The most basic and immediate instrumental needs—such as food, heat, and housing—take priority over more complex intrapsychic and interpersonal problems. Having families prioritize their concerns not only teaches them a skill but also conveys the message that they are capable, strong, and best know their own needs. If a counselor determines needs without consulting the family, the family once again gets the message that it is incompetent. If the family does not perceive itself as having the problems the counselor identifies, change is unlikely to occur. The counselor cannot have a preconceived notion of what a family needs. Having the family define its needs increases the likelihood of a trusting relationship between worker and family.

Finding Strengths

Assessments focus on health, not pathology. A counselor identifies family strengths and builds on these through interventions. Although families have many problems, they also possess strengths, which have often been over-looked by those who have worked with them in the past. A counselor looks for "threads of health on which to build. . . . In the old records, strengths are buried under a heap of pathology; but if you look intently enough, they emerge."[1]

Focusing on a family's weaknesses without considering its assets makes it impossible for a counselor to initiate a trusting relationship. Building on family strengths benefits both the family and the family worker: it helps the counselor overcome the human service profession's view that the family is hopeless and assists the family in altering the way it views itself. Emphasizing strengths helps both the family and the family worker be more optimistic about the possibility of change. Unlike previous family workers, this counselor believes in the family, and recognizes that it has strengths and can change.

Giving Hope

Assessments are structured to give families hope. They do not involve statements such as, "you need to stop being depressed." Problems are resolved in small, feasible steps. For a depressed individual, to try to "stop being depressed" is an overwhelming, unmanageable, and unrealistic goal, and sets the stage for failure. Goals such as getting up in the morning and taking a shower are achievable expectations that have a higher probability of success.

Helping families achieve small successes with concrete problems provides them with renewed hope. The following case is an example. Truancy is not an uncommon problem in the Rossi family. Cindy has been truant since the beginning of the year; she claims that school bores her. Mrs. Rossi, who never graduated from high school, tries in every way possible to convince Cindy to attend school, but to no avail. Mrs. Rossi finally gives up, considering both herself and her daughter failures. The family worker refuses to accept this hopeless attitude, and brings Mrs. Rossi and Cindy to the school principal. Together, they decide to change Cindy's schedule so that she takes only the major subjects and has only five hours of schooling a day. Cindy is delighted with the schedule change and attends school regularly. Mrs. Rossi cannot believe the enormous effect that this change has on her daughter. For the first time, Mrs. Rossi is able to admit that one should never give up hope. Furthermore, she is willing to pursue counseling.

Providing Treatment Alternatives

The family counselor defines the presenting problem so that it can be resolved. To expand treatment alternatives, family problems are viewed as deficits of skills. It is easier for someone to increase a skill than to stop a negative behavior. For example, "Mrs. Mahoney needs to develop ways to handle her anger" is easier to work on than "Mrs. Mahoney is a very hateful woman who takes her anger out on her daughter."

Good assessments do not involve negative labeling, such as, "Mr. Tobias is a hopeless alcoholic." Such an assessment assumes that there are no treatment options. If stated, "Mr. Tobias has problems with alcohol that affect his ability to parent," the problem is amenable to change, and treatment possibilities are expanded to include involvement in Alcoholics Anonymous, Parent Effectiveness Training, or a parent support group.

An assessment such as, "Mrs. Mueller has no control over her children" limits treatment options to, "tell her to take some control." Treatment alternatives are generated when the assessment expands rather than limits options. A better assessment is, "Mrs. Mueller tries to discipline her children and is unable to succeed." This assessment opens up possibilities for intervention, such as assertiveness training, a parent support group, behavior management, discussing her feelings of hopelessness, building Mrs. Mueller's self-confidence, determining Mr. Mueller's role in disciplining the children, and learning about Mrs. Mueller's formal and informal support systems. Defining problems from a few different perspectives will help expand treatment alternatives.[2]

Considering the Family's Culture: Implications for Minority Families

Too often a family's culture and values are overlooked. A counselor needs to understand a family's ethnic and cultural background. A program serving minorities hires family workers who represent the target population. It is particularly necessary to hire such workers to help families that have not learned to speak English. The Lower East Side Family Union in New York, for example, works with a diverse ethnic population, in which most families are Hispanic and Chinese. Bilingual staff are familiar with the culture and ethnicity of the families served, and often live within the local community.

Minority children represent a disproportionate percentage of the youth in substitute care. Twenty-two percent of the youths in institutions and 36 percent of the youths in substitute care are black, whereas blacks make up only 13.6 percent of the youth population.[3] Children from American Indian, Hispanic, and poor families also constitute a disproportionate percentage of youths in out-of-home placement. In their *Annotated Bibliography on Family Based Services,* the National Resource Center on Family Based Services lists publications that address minority issues. In addition, the center's publication, *Placement Prevention and Family Reunification: A Handbook for the Family-Centered Service Practitioner* reviews service delivery issues in working with black, Hispanic, Indo-Chinese, and Native American families.

Examining Sources of Support and Stress within the Family and the Community

It is important to distinguish between the family's two roles: those within the family and those outside of the family. The counselor assesses intrafamilial roles and also the degree to which family members are integrated in the larger social system, such as the neighborhood, community, peer group, school, and workplace. "A child with a problem cannot be seen as the sole repository of his problems, nor necessarily should his family. A mental health professional must look at the context of the child with all its ecosystems."[4]

A number of authors emphasize the importance of assessing the family within the many systems with which it interfaces.[5] Conceptualizing the family in its ecological context or environment expands treatment options. The counselor examines the sources of support and stress for family members within all its interfacing systems. For example, a family worker finds that the mother in a single-parent family believes she must always stay at home with her children; she rarely goes out with friends. A primary treatment goal is to increase the mother's involvement with her peers through participation in a mother's group. This provides an invaluable source of support for a woman whose cultural values discourage individual independence.

If, when assessing a family, a counselor sees potential sources of support for family members within the family itself, he or she encourages their development. For example, Karen is successful at making friends, whereas her sister, Deborah, has great difficulty making friends and is isolated. The counselor, seeing that Karen takes an interest in her younger sister and is willing to help her, commends Karen on her ability to make friends easily and asks her to share her knowledge with her sister.

6
Diagnostic Tools

Certain diagnostic tools aid the counselor in conducting assessments. This chapter discusses the benefits of in-home assessment, the importance of defining family structure, the identification of detouring, and the examination of developmental stages of family members.

Conducting an In-Home Assessment

When initiating a relationship with a multiproblem family, a counselor makes a strong effort to establish a rapport with a family that feels untrusting, angry at the "helping" profession, and defeated. The counselor begins building a relationship by meeting the family in its home.[1]

Conducting an in-home assessment indicates to the family that the counselor has gone out of his or her way to meet the family on its own turf. The entire family and significant others are more easily involved in the meeting. Home visits automatically include all family members. "Accepting the family's turf is no guarantee that you will succeed in engaging everyone in treatment, but it does improve the chances."[2]

Family members typically feel more secure and more in control in meetings in their home; they have greater confidence and their resistance diminishes. In-home assessments enable a counselor to understand the family's physical environment and acquire a more realistic picture of the family's lifestyle than can be obtained at an office. Do people regularly stop in to see the family, without calling first? Does the telephone ring all evening? Does the physical living space permit family members to find privacy? These questions are best answered through an in-home assessment.

Assessing Family Structure

In diagnosing a family, the counselor examines family structure. What are the preferred transactional patterns in the family? Does a child refuse to answer questions and let the father answer for him or her? Is this a pattern in the family? If so, the pattern will be repeated, giving the counselor more than one opportunity to notice it. After assessing family structure, the counselor devises alternative responses that family members can employ to improve their situation. The counselor also determines the family's flexibility and capacity for restructuring its familiar patterns.

The following case indicates the importance of assessing family structure. The Kennedy family includes Mrs. Kennedy, her four children (aged twenty-one, twelve, eight, and three), and Mrs. Kennedy's mother. During family meetings, the family worker observes that Paul, the youngest boy, who is twelve, constantly interrupts his mother and tries to divert her attention. Mrs. Kennedy attempts to control Paul, but to no avail. Even when the family worker meets with Mrs. Kennedy alone, they are continuously interrupted by Paul, who runs in and out of the house. Each time Paul enters, he has something "important" to tell his mother. He ignores the family worker, refusing to acknowledge that his mother is in the middle of a conversation. Having been interrupted repeatedly, the counselor asks Mrs. Kennedy to control her son. Despite this direct request, Mrs. Kennedy remains unable to control Paul. The counselor intervenes and gets the situation under control, with the knowledge that one of the goals in working with this family is to help the mother learn how to set limits with her son.

Is There Detouring?

When conducting an assessment, the counselor determines if there is detouring in the family. For example, is stress in the marital relationship inappropriately diverted to the children? The real stress (in the marriage) may be manifested by a child who is shoplifting and lying (the symptoms). The symptom-bearer is the lesser of two evils within the family system; he or she is "saving" the parents' marriage. Stress between husband and wife may be too difficult for them to confront, thus their problems are expressed through the child's acting out. Focusing on the child unites them around a common concern. Without this commonality or bond, they may find they have little reason to stay together.

The following case shows how detouring is expressed within the family system. Money has been a longstanding source of conflict between Mr. O'Keefe and his daughter, Thea. Mr. O'Keefe gives Thea a weekly allowance, but she constantly complains that it is not enough. When Thea is caught shoplifting, her father confronts her and she denies her actions; yet the episode repeats itself again and again, until Thea has no choice but to admit that she shoplifts. Then her father learns that his wife gives Thea money whenever she asks for it. During a family session, Thea unexpectedly says that ever since her parents started fighting and arguing, she has been going into stores and taking whatever catches her eye. She realizes that her mother gives her money as a way to anger her father, but she is never able to spend the money because she considers it a bribe—something not meant to be spent. Mr. and Mrs. O'Keefe, quite surprised by this discovery, are willing to confront the problem. Mr. O'Keefe agrees to raise Thea's allowance, and promises to be more flexible in accommodating her needs; Mrs. O'Keefe agrees to stop giving Thea money on an irregular basis. Husband and wife acknowledge their need for marital counseling.

Examining Developmental Stages

The counselor examines the normal developmental stage for each family member, to see if each member's behavior is appropriate for his or her stage. For example, why is Fran, age ten, spending all her leisure time at home with her mother, rather than with children her own age?

Parents set rules that are age-appropriate when their children are young, but sometimes fail to realize that these rules need to change as children grow older. A developmental change that commonly precipitates family problems is the child's entry into adolescence. At this time, the youngster's extrafamilial activities increase, and the relationship between adolescent and parents changes. An adolescent needs to be set apart from siblings and given the increased freedom and responsibility that is appropriate at adolescence. The interactions with the parental subsystem must change from parents-child to parents-adolescent. If parents are inflexible, and do not acknowledge their youngster's transition to adolescence and the need to change relationships within the family, conflict ensues.

The following case illustrates the importance of recognizing and acknowledging developmental stages. Curfew time in the Jenkins household is 8:30 P.M. Pam, fourteen, Ron, eleven, and Don, seven, have to be in bed at the same time. Pam rebels by repeatedly running away from home and staying at friends' houses without notifying her parents. When the family is referred to a social service agency, Pam is on the run. During family meetings, the question of curfew is raised, and it becomes apparent that Mr. and Mrs. Jenkins set very rigid limitations on their children. The family worker discusses this with the parents who, at first, are unable to see that their rules are overly strict. Eventually, however, they are willing to make some changes. They realize that they must consider their children as individuals who have different needs at different points in their development.

7

Intervention Strategies

F amily counseling programs serving multiproblem families use a variety of treatment modalities. Before examining these specific modalities, the counselor must first consider the needs of the families to be served and understand overall strategies that are effective, regardless of which treatment modality is employed.

For the most part, multiproblem families operate on a concrete level, are action-oriented, and have little desire to verbalize. Thus, these families are not responsive to insight therapy. Several general strategies are recommended in the following sections.

Empowering the Family

Developing a Partnership

Although a counselor has many goals while working with a family, the overriding goal is to empower the family to become autonomous, independent, and able to meet its own needs. From the very beginning, a counselor prepares the family for the time when it will be on its own. Encouraging a dependent relationship is counterproductive, because the counselor's involvement is time-limited.

The relationship between counselor and family is a partnership characterized by mutual respect and collaboration. It is unproductive for a family worker to dictate treatment goals. For too long social workers have assumed that families, especially multiproblem families, are incapable of understanding their problems. Treatment based on this philosophy is oxymoronic. How can a social worker who enters a family for the first time assume that his or her assessment of this family's problems is more valid than the opinions of the family members, which are based on years of experience of relationships among family members. Treatment is based on the family's goals. A family is its own best resource, yet this obvious fact is often overlooked.

A counselor encourages family members to participate fully in treatment; they feel a part of the process, and do not regard it as "something happening to them." To build a family's trust, the counselor may show the family its file, which indicates that the counselor is working with family members, not reporting on them. Empowerment occurs at every level of treatment; it can be subtle or obvious, but the family must have no doubt that the counselor believes they are capable and can become autonomous.

Providing a Model Relationship

The counselor-family relationship is of tantamount importance.[1] A national survey of family-centered programs conducted by the National Resource Center on Family Based Services in Iowa revealed that the most important component of effective service is the counselor-family relationship.[2] Jones, Magura, and Shyne concur with this finding, reporting that numerous studies recognize the counselor-family relationship as intrinsic to the provision of effective service.[3] Success hinges on the development of a relationship that is characterized by the counselor's respect for the family and confidence in its ability to make changes. Some family members may never have had positive, trusting relationships, and although it is a difficult undertaking, the counselor develops such a relationship. This process may entail arriving at a family's house and finding them not at home, or being the target of a family member's anger and frustration at other social workers with whom they were involved. Despite initial rejection, the counselor returns to work with the family. The fact that the counselor comes back, despite incredible resistance, is significant to the family.

The counselor's concern and insistence on working with the family are fundamental to the development of a family-counselor partnership. Being accepting, accessible, reliable, and consistent, and communicating a sense of caring are crucial qualities of the counselor. Maintaining patience, being persistent, overcoming a family's resistance, and working with family members who are distrustful, angry, and defeated is a challenge in the strongest sense of the word.

When initiating a relationship with a family, the counselor focuses on the parents rather than the children, because changes in family dynamics are reinforced by the parents. By addressing the family's concrete needs, as well as their emotional needs, the counselor gains their trust. Because parents were deprived in their childhoods, the counselor provides the nurturing they failed to receive from their own parents. Thus, the family worker reparents the parents, providing them with understanding, consistency, and support. "Through their relationship with the worker, parents find someone that they can depend on, decreasing their need to depend upon their own children in unhealthy and inappropriate ways."[4] Parents need to meet their own needs effectively before they can meet those of their children. Through the counselor-parent relationship, the worker demonstrates or models healthy parenting skills. Reeducation and reparenting are essential elements of the relationship.

Once a trusting, reciprocal relationship is established, the family has faith in the counselor and believes that he or she is looking out for the family's best interests. This relationship serves as a model for the family and guides family members in their relationships among themselves and with the community.

Putting Parents in Charge

Parents are the most important people in a child's life. They are put in charge from the very beginning of treatment, and participate in planning and decision making throughout treatment. Sometimes parents have no control over their child; they do not know how to set limits. They may, on the other hand, be too controlling, thereby not permitting their child to become independent. Working closely with parents takes the focus off the identified client and benefits the family as a whole. Skills learned by parents benefit all of the children, not just the identified client. The more competent and self-confident the parent(s), the healthier the children.

Parents may feel powerless and regard the world as hostile; they may lack the energy and self-confidence to overcome their difficulties. Although many parents attempt to resolve their dilemmas, they often feel paralyzed. In single-parent households, the parent with whom the child resides is usually the mother. Single mothers require much support, such as financial assistance, day care, vocational training, or education in life skills. A mother may be overwhelmed by her children and unaware of how to gain control over her own life. Besides providing a sympathetic ear, the counselor assists the mother in gaining access to community resources. Enhancing the mother's self-esteem and developing her confidence in her ability to provide for her family are critical.

Emphasizing the Positive: Building on Strengths

The counselor must look for firm areas within the family's structure on which to build.[5] Although social work professes to emphasize enhancing family strengths, such a focus is uncommon. Considering a family's assets, resources, and abilities to cope assumes a recognition of how the family is helping itself. A counselor operating from this standpoint facilitates treatment from a positive (healthy) rather than a negative (pathological) framework, which expands problem-solving options.

Each family member possesses certain strengths that may be hidden or overlooked. The counselor emphasizes, reinforces, and enhances these strengths. This approach contributes to the development of self-confidence, inspires hope, and promotes growth within the family. Indications of positive change are recognized and progress is reinforced, which encourages continued family improvement.

Besides building on family strengths, the counselor reframes negative statements by giving them new names that change the value of the patterns. For example, if a mother says that her son is doing poorly in school and that she has told him again and again to improve his grades, the counselor does not call this mother controlling. Instead, the counselor reframes her attitude as concern for her son. Reframing occurs throughout treatment.

Frequent Contact and Accessibility

Family counselors are on call twenty-four hours a day, seven days a week.[6] This shows families that staff are accessible and that assistance is not limited to a one-hour-per-week therapy session. Constant availability, frequent telephone contact, and home visits by the counselor help solidify the relationship between the counselor and the family. In many traditional programs, staff are inaccessible at the times a family most needs assistance. Clients feel secure knowing their counselors are available. At the beginning of family counseling, clients may call family workers often. As a family progresses through counseling, the family members develop their own coping mechanisms, and learn to postpone gratification and to manage crises.

Using Action-Oriented, Concrete, Problem-Solving Strategies

The counselor does not simply employ "talking" therapy with multiproblem families, but uses a style that involves action. Interventions such as sculpting and manipulation of space are used. Sculpting is useful in both diagnosis and treatment, because it brings issues into the foreground and provides a family with a visible, concrete understanding of its structure. Action therapy is effective because an act, unlike words, will not go away. Since multiproblem families operate more on a concrete level than a process level, interventions that complement "talk therapy" are employed. Concrete interventions are used as a basis for discussion. If, for example, the counselor does not think that the husband and wife are close, he or she physically moves the wife's chair next to her husband's. The way the couple responds to this change (intervention) provides the counselor with further diagnostic material. This is an example of manipulation of space.

The counselor instructs family members to conduct task-oriented, interpersonal exercises. For example, if a father is perceived as a peripheral family member, the counselor asks him to choose, with his son, an activity that they both enjoy and to plan a specific time to undertake the activity together. This interpersonal exercise is both task-oriented and concrete. The task chosen is not important; achieving the desired result of bringing father and son closer is primary.

The following case shows the importance of concrete, task-oriented interventions that are monitored in counselor-family meetings. Donna Quill enjoys cooking and baking, but is unable to relax in the presence of her mother. Mrs. Quill, a divorcee who once worked as a cook, has always wanted to teach cookery to her daughter, but consistently finds herself arguing with Donna over trivial matters. Since Thanksgiving is approaching and both Mrs. Quill and Donna are looking forward to a family gathering at their house, the family worker suggests that Donna and her mother prepare a meal together. Their first reactions are resistance and objection, but the counselor adds the provision that neither Mrs. Quill nor Donna be in the kitchen at the same time, and they agree to the plan. The arrangement works smoothly, and through meetings with their counselor they learn how to better communicate.

The more concrete, action-oriented interventions are employed, the more effective the counseling will be. For example, rather than simply discussing relationships in a family, the counselor can draw a diagram illustrating the issue under discussion.

Emphasizing the Present

Counseling emphasizes the here and now. The worker addresses the immediate, most pressing needs of the family, such as housing, health care, child care, or the need for a job. When a family worker talks with a family, the focus is on the present: the counselor and the family do not talk in abstract terms about what is happening. Instead, the counselor helps the family act out what is happening. "To achieve the optimal tension levels, we try whenever possible to transform a conflict that is talked about into a conflict that is happening now and to shift the level of intervention from talking about past events toward resolving a felt tension in the present conflict."[7] Family members tend to talk to the counselor about a problem, instead of communicating directly. The counselor instructs individuals to speak directly to each other, which makes the discussion more immediate and more real. For example, a mother, who is angry at her son for regularly missing school and coming home late at night, complains to the counselor about her son. The counselor instructs the mother to speak directly to her son, so that her anger is channeled in the proper direction and the action is brought into the present.

It is relatively easy for individuals to talk about their problems; enacting the problems puts family members much more in touch with the pressing issues. At the same time, the counselor can observe the interactions and immediately intervene to restructure dysfunctional patterns. Emphasizing the present rather than focusing on past patterns "acknowledge(s) that past behavior is part of the old pattern and does not necessarily indicate the only possibility of which the participants are capable. This is an optimistic attitude, usually accurate, which keeps the focus on health, with its constant options and potentials for change, rather than on the compelling pressures of the past, which justify pathology as inevitable and therefore unchangeable."[8]

Concentrate on Process, Not Content

Because a family provides a counselor with extensive information, the counselor is in danger of becoming overwhelmed with data. To observe the process (recurring patterns) without getting stuck on content is the counselor's focus. Patterns that are significant in a family will happen more than once. A counselor looks for patterns that recur (process), regardless of the information being discussed (content). For example, when Kathy speaks, she is repeatedly interrupted or mocked by her two younger sisters. This occurs no matter what Kathy tries to discuss. The process (patterns) rather than the content (subject matter) is important.

Behavioral Change, Not Insight

Whatever originally triggered a problem does not necessarily account for its current existence. It is not necessary to analyze why the problem began and how it unfolded, or to obtain extensive understanding of the situation. A family does not have to be aware of the process (the acts that contribute to the presenting problem) to understand the outcome. Issues are addressed on a conscious level, and the goal of counseling is structural change that will extinguish symptoms—not insight.

Observe, Hypothesize, Experiment

A counselor observes family interactions, hypothesizes about which interventions are likely to succeed, and experiments with interventions to restructure the family system. The counselor often shares his or her observations with the family and asks if they are willing to try a new way of responding. Each experiment provides additional diagnostic material. When interventions are introduced, the counselor can observe how family members react to change (stress placed on the system). Do they integrate it? Deflect it? Reject it?

It is unrealistic for a counselor to expect all interventions to succeed. Whether an intervention is rejected or integrated, the family worker's understanding of the family is enhanced. Sometimes an intervention fails because it is inappropriate, or because the family is not ready to integrate the intervention at that time, even though they may be able to do so in the future.

An Ecological Approach: Using Community Resources with the Worker as Advocate

Because he or she appreciates the importance of the family's social environment, a counselor initiates contact with people who are significantly involved with the family, in order to obtain a thorough understanding of the family. This approach insures coordinated treatment. The counselor maintains contact with these significant people. In addition, the counselor assists the family in using community resources. Accessing and working closely and cooperatively with community resources is fundamental to a program's success. Neither one family counselor nor a team of counselors can be all things to a multiproblem family.

Having established a strong relationship with a family, the worker then teaches family members how to use community resources to meet their needs.[9] Rather than simply referring the family to a resource, the counselor accompanies them there, and acts as both role model and advocate.

Before they use a resource, the counselor prepares the family members. For example, if a child is referred to a play therapy group, the parents need to understand the relevance of play therapy. Often a counselor needs to do considerable work with the family before they are ready for referral. If referrals are made before a family is motivated to make real use of them, the services will not help. The counselor must also prepare the service to which a family is referred, in order to insure that the family is well received. A primary goal of treatment is to generalize the trusting relationship between the counselor and the family, so that the family develops a positive attitude toward community agencies.

8
Termination

Termination of the counselor-family relationship is often completely overlooked, or at best underemphasized, by human service agencies. A counselor and a family establish a highly involved relationship, and a family worker realizes the importance of a careful, well-planned termination.

The family actively participates in deciding when and how the termination will occur; this decision is not made by the counselor alone. Positive termination occurs when a family is stable and coping well, when a child is no longer at risk of placement, and when the family has a network of supportive services, both formal and informal, in place. Negative termination is appropriate when the family, counselor, and referral source agree that the services have been ineffectual; or when the family refuses to participate in the program, despite efforts by staff to involve family members; or when more drastic treatment is required to safeguard a child or parent's safety.

Unfortunately, their funding sources sometimes pressure programs to terminate prematurely, so that they can serve other families. In the intensive, time-limited treatment model, the family and the counselor both know when termination will occur. It is an advantage for termination to be predetermined by the program design because it puts treatment into temporal perspective.

A counselor begins the termination process at the start of treatment. Family members understand that the worker will help them build their competence until they are able to do so for themselves. Family members need a support system beyond the family itself. Termination occurs when the family is able to meet its own needs, effectively cope with crises, and successfully access community resources.

Because the family and the counselor have a strong relationship, termination is difficult; yet it is essential for termination to be handled smoothly. Once a termination date has been set, family members often respond with anxiety, sadness, regression, anger, distance (by canceling appointments), or acting out. The family needs assistance in addressing its anxiety about termination.

Before terminating with a family, the counselor must be certain that symptom substitution has not occurred within the family. Often, one part of a system becomes dysfunctional when another improves. For example, Melinda, fifteen, stops missing school and throwing temper tantrums, but her younger brother, Tom, age nine, previously a quiet child, begins behaving as Maria had previously. Thus, the symptom appears in another family member. Real change within the family system occurs when the symptom goes away and no one else in the family takes up the function (symptom).

To keep families from becoming dependent on their counselors, most programs provide intensive services while concommitantly involving families with the community resources they need. Thereby, families learn how to meet their needs in the community, and at the same time gradually decrease their dependence on the program.

When terminating, it is useful for the counselor to gradually extend the time between family meetings (once a week, every two weeks, once a month); this enables the family to slowly lessen their involvement in the program. The family grows more self-reliant, but the counselor is still available to provide assistance as necessary. In the last few family meetings, the family worker and the family look back on what they have accomplished since they started. The counselor reinforces family successes and supports their desire to maintain the changes. The worker also conveys confidence in the family's ability to further develop its strengths.

Termination is a joint endeavor between the counselor and the family. It gives a counselor the opportunity to ask family members what they thought of program interventions. What was useful? What was not? What could have been done better? The counselor obtains feedback, and at the same time affirms the family's ability to be authoritative, assertive, and participatory. Counseling encourages family members to respect themselves; termination reinforces the family's competence and their belief in the value of their opinions.

Termination is recognized by a formal celebration held to signify that a family has successfully terminated its dependence on the counselor. This ceremony further reinforces the family's progress and conveys a belief in the family's ability to continue to succeed. Giving the family something tangible like a certificate or a gift, such as a plant, is a concrete way for the counselor to remind them of the counseling experience. A plant is an appropriate gift because it will grow, like a family, but any gift can serve the same purpose.

9
Staff

Family counseling programs employ professional staff, paraprofessional staff, or a combination of both. The quality of the staff recruited is critical to a program's success. Degrees are unimportant; staff must understand multiproblem families, believe that these families can be empowered, recognize that resistance will be great and rewards slow in coming, and, most importantly, be willing to do whatever is necessary to assist these families. ·

Staff must be willing to "roll up their sleeves," to provide concrete and psychological services. They must also be willing to devote a good deal of time and energy to their jobs; to grow, change, and take risks; and to employ innovative treatment strategies. They must be patient, resourceful, and able to cope with high levels of stress. A sense of humor is fundamental!

The Advantages of Paraprofessional Staff

Paraprofessionals are known as community workers, mental health workers, or parent aides. They are a vital, yet largely invisible, manpower resource in the delivery of mental health services; they comprise either all or part of the staffs of many family counseling programs. The direct service staff of some programs are entirely paraprofessionals; other programs have paraprofessionals and professionals working together as a team.

There are many advantages to employing paraprofessionals to work with multiproblem families. Many paraprofessionals have faced problems similar to those of the families they serve; their competence is based on experience rather than theory. Their personal experience gives them an intuitive wisdom that, tempered by professional supervision, enormously enhances their ability to help. Because they are not hindered by theoretical training, paraprofessionals are more easily able to relate to their clients. "Programs using paraprofessional home visitors have repeatedly found that these visitors were less threatening and more easily accepted than more highly trained persons who shared fewer common experiences with their clients."[1] Families respect and respond to the fact that their counselors have "made it," and such family workers convey the belief that the families can make it too. "The clients' knowledge that they were being helped by people who had had to overcome severe privations in their own lives helped to ease the defensiveness against the helping person."[2] The paraprofessionals' intuition helps them avoid the pitfalls encountered by a professional counselor, who may address subtle problems before resolving simple ones and may involve clients with too many service providers without guaranteeing a single positive service.

As a result of their personal experiences, paraprofessionals are adept at utilizing community resources and avoiding the bureaucratic responses that deny service to those who cannot comprehend vague and intricate procedures. Paraprofessionals not only assist families in obtaining needed services, they also commiserate with them, thereby establishing a quick rapport.

The advantages of employing paraprofessional staff are numerous, but there are also drawbacks. Paraprofessionals tend to become overinvolved with families, and often have trouble differentiating themselves from their clients. They must recognize that they cannot be everything to the families they serve, and that, instead, they must empower the families to help themselves. Paraprofessionals require extensive support and continual supervision; they also need assistance in improving their clinical skills. They are often intuitively knowledgeable but need to gain an understanding of why their work is effectual or ineffectual.

The preceding discussion of the advantages of paraprofessional staff does not insinuate that professionals are less capable of working with multiproblem families. The importance of paraprofessionals is stressed for two reasons. First, it is appalling that the strengths of paraprofessionals are often overlooked, minimized, or discussed in a derogatory manner. Paraprofessionals are often underpayed and victimized by sex discrimination (many paraprofessionals are females). In the literature as well as in a number of operational programs, paraprofessionals are treated as second class. Often the paraprofessional is called a "nonprofessional." In many programs a professional is teamed with a paraprofessional, yet the hierarchy is apparent. The paraprofessional is responsible for home management, transportation, day care, and other concrete needs, whereas the professional concentrates on the therapy. Second, individuals with master's degrees are often disinterested in work with multiproblem families. For the most part, professionals have been trained in traditional settings and in traditional casework; many obtained their degrees in order to establish private practices and receive third-party payments. The financial reward is not an incentive for working with multiproblem families.

How to Support and Keep Staff: The Importance of Training and Supervision

The Benefits of Training and Supervision

Staff training and supervision are critical to program efficacy. Staff participate in an orientation to become familiar with the program's philosophy, gain an understanding of the target population, learn about assessment and intervention strategies, and become acquainted with the local human service delivery system. This type of preservice training is the minimum offered; depending on the type of staff employed, more extensive initial training may be necessary.

Continued training and supervision increases motivation, inspires creativity, and decreases burnout. Working with multiproblem families is emotionally intense, time-consuming, and stressful; families are resistant and progress is slow. Staff need frequent demonstrations of support through regular individual and/or group supervision. Such support not only helps workers, it also insures that families receive quality services.

This continuing inservice training is designed to address issues that present clinical and programmatic problems. The training is concrete and practical, rather than abstract and theoretical; participants obtain skills and concepts that they can apply directly to their work. Trainers are brought to the program; staff train in the areas in which they are expert; and if the program is part of a larger agency, agency staff offer training. A program may use its training money to bring in consultants who are experts in a variety of fields, so that staff can obtain training in specific subject areas. Staff are also encouraged to take advantage of training outside of the agency.

The state of Maine provides a special course for the staff of its family preservation programs. Each year this training takes different forms. In 1983, staff met one day per month for nine months (a total of sixty hours) to receive training in home-based family counseling and discuss cases. As an outgrowth of this course, program participants voluntarily decided to meet one day each month to provide mutual support. In 1985, Maine held a five-day residential training program, followed by monthly inservice training sessions. The training focused on family dynamics and techniques, and on how to recognize when families require additional expertise and how to access this.[3]

Supervisory Skills

In some programs, individual and/or group supervision is offered by the program director or a consultant; others rely on peer supervision. Any, all, or a combination of these forms of supervision may occur. Peer supervision is especially useful because it offers counselors the opportunity to share ideas, discuss difficult cases, and learn from each other, and provides support, encouragement, and a strong common bond.

The importance of a good clinical supervisor cannot be overstated. A well-trained clinician supports, oversees, and teaches his or her staff. Supervisors not only focus on the families served, they also help family workers recognize their own needs. Through supervision, counselors come to understand the structures and dynamics of their own families. For example, a counselor from an alcoholic family might have difficulty working with an alcoholic family until he or she acknowledges and addresses the lingering issues from his or her own upbringing.

Staff must feel that their supervisor is both approachable and available. It is particularly important that he or she is accessible to family workers in crisis situations. If a counselor feels intimidated or uncomfortable around his or her supervisor, the counselor may try to single-handedly handle a crisis that is too overwhelming. The supervisor must feel comfortable about inter-acting directly with families, and must be willing to work with them in their homes. "If social workers are to be truly effective social intervenors, they must be willing to get their hands dirty again. They must be willing to go into the ghettos and *barrios* and to work with families whose styles of com-munication, organization, and participation do not fit the social mold."[4] Personal, on-the-spot supervision enhances the counselor's work and helps the supervisor maintain a realistic perspective on the demands of the work.

A supervisor recognizes the achievements of staff and acknowledges their skills. Counselors cannot look to the families they serve for recognition; they must obtain it from their supervisor and their peers. The supervisor encour-ages staff to rely on their own resources, intuition, and knowledge when working with families. Each counselor develops his or her own style.

Some counselors repeatedly ask their supervisors how to handle certain situations. The supervisor helps such counselors solve problems by creating a variety of alternatives; giving counselors "the answer" does not help them learn. In this way, staff are like their clients, who want someone to tell them exactly what to do. A supervisor's method of supervision is analogous to the way counselors work with families. The supervisor gently pushes staff, recognizes their strengths, helps them solve problems and encourages them to search for their own solutions.

Peer support is also critical to program success. The program director encourages such support through the development of an esprit de corps. An environment in which staff feel a sense of belonging, commitment to their work, and appreciation by others is optimal. Counselors need to be com-fortable with each other and know that they can rely on one another for mutual support, advice, and recognition.

Preventing Burnout

The "personality" of a family counseling program either contributes to or obviates burnout. The program director may unrealistically expect staff to dedicate their lives to the program; although this philosophy is never ver-balized, it is understood. This attitude encourages burnout, causes compe-tition among staff, and creates an unhealthy work environment. A program director should be sensitive to counselors' workloads and encourage them to maintain a balance between their work and their personal lives.

Burnout can be prevented in a number of ways. Recognizing staff is one method; recognition can take the form of offering opportunities for promotion, paying good salaries, or providing excellent learning opportunities. Maine is considering a plan to partially subsidize the master's degrees of staff who sign a two-year contract. This plan makes positions attractive, encourages a two-year commitment, and guarantees staff the opportunity for educational advancement. Another way to prevent burnout is to involve staff in decision making. Giving staff a say in the program's direction gives them power, recognizes the value of their opinions, fosters personal investment in the program, and enhances staff commitment.

10
Program Evaluation

If family therapy is to be recognized as a viable treatment alternative, more and better-controlled comparative studies of the results must be conducted. The quality and quantity of the research on the effectiveness of family therapy has so far been disappointing.[1] Much of the research is methodologically unsound, shaky, or open to interpretation. Treatment efficacy and cost effectiveness seem promising, yet more rigorous research needs to be conducted.

Evaluation is neglected throughout the social service profession; this tendency is not unique to family preservation programs. Essentially, two factors account for this lack of emphasis on evaluation. First and most important, funding is usually not allocated to determining program efficacy. Unless a program develops its own in-house evaluation, none is conducted. Most funding sources fail to recognize the importance of evaluation; they usually require minimal evaluation and rarely fund analyses of the program's long-term impact. For funding sources, program evaluation is tied to funding decisions; such evaluations are not concerned with which interventions work and why. Funding sources may want to know if a program has met its goals, but often these goals are either vague or elementary. The second main reason for lack of evaluation is that human service staff are often inexperienced or unconcerned with evaluation; their priority is direct service. Most staff do not know how to design an evaluation, and in many cases, staff are intimidated by evaluation because they consider the topic too esoteric to grasp.

Working in family preservation programs is taxing, and staff time is consumed by direct service. Little or no time is allocated for evaluation. Social service professionals must be educated about the importance of evaluation. Perhaps this education needs to begin with funding sources, who can make program evaluation a priority by providing funding. Until this happens, much can be done by agencies. Program directors can recognize the necessity of evaluations, and can impart an understanding of their importance to staff. Establishing an in-house evaluation of one's own family preservation program is at least a beginning.

A program's stated objectives provide the basis for what to evaluate. As a first step, programs need to define clear, concrete, measurable program objectives. Programs can measure changes in families and identify effective intervention strategies. Any program can implement this minimal level of evaluation.

Evaluation is a continuing process. A framework for measuring program efficacy must be established so that client progress can be monitored at regular intervals. Evaluation is also an interactive process that, like treatment, involves a partnership between counselor and family. Unfortunately, the family is often an untapped resource; family members are best able to say which interventions they found most and least useful. The family's role in program evaluation is most important.

We need to conduct more comparative studies using control groups (groups with characteristics as similar as possible to program participants, but who do not receive services). Control group studies are the most effective program evaluations, but for practical and political reasons they are difficult to implement. Although such studies are costly and time-consuming, they greatly contribute to our knowledge.

Most program evaluations are qualitative rather than quantitative; qualitative evidence includes self-reports by families and case studies. Although quantitative evaluations are much more difficult to conduct, both qualitative and quantitative evaluations are useful. We must not limit ourselves to qualitative evaluations.

Most program evaluations are not rigorous, and are short-term, not long-term. Families are not usually followed after they have terminated from a program; if they are monitored, it is typically for only a year. More data on long-term results would be advantageous. A major obstacle to long-term follow-up is that many multiproblem families move regularly and do not have telephones, so that it is difficult and often impossible to locate them.

Most evaluations measure the outcomes for children rather than changes in family systems. Social work has a history of working with individuals, not families. Although family preservation programs focus on the family rather than on the identified client, the evaluations of many of these programs continue to measure change in the identified client.[2] We must dispense with such a narrow focus and expand evaluations to encompass behavioral and attitudinal change within the family and between the family and the community. Evaluation must catch up with treatment by moving from a limited emphasis on the outcomes for children to a systems perspective.

A number of instruments measure changes in the knowledge, skills, and/or attitudes of individuals; these include testing, project-designed inventory scales, checklists, and attitudinal surveys. An evaluator can choose validated instruments for measurement or can design evaluation tools tailored to specific program objectives. Although instruments that assess individual change assist in determining program efficacy, to comprehensively evaluate programs we must develop instruments that measure changes in families and that consider them in the context of their communities. Is a family less socially isolated after program intervention? Is a family able to utilize community resources to meet its needs? Does the relationship between family and community change?

Most home-based, family-centered programs define success according to one or two criteria: in terms of the number of times placement has been averted and in terms of whether the identified client is involved in the activities that initiated the referral. Although this information is important, it does not help us understand why a program is effective. We need to determine which intervention strategies work, and with what types of people. Until this information is obtained, we will not know why our programs are successful and we will have no hard data on which to base the development of future programs.

Program evaluations need to research the processes as well as the outcomes of treatment.[3] A process evaluation considers the different parts of a program and how they are linked; it entails careful, systematic documentation of the project's attributes, clients, and service provision. An outcome evaluation considers how closely the outcomes of a program match the stated goals. When a problem is identified, a theory about the best way to address the problem is chosen; program goals and services are based on this theory. An outcome evaluation measures changes in the target population, and determines the extent to which program services, in themselves, created these changes. Process and outcome evaluations, employed together, provide a balanced program analysis.

Program evaluations must not only collect data that substantiate effective intervention strategies; they must also compare the results of family support programs to the results of placement in institutional settings and residential and foster care. Qualitative as well as quantitative variables must be compared, as well as cost effectiveness and the long-term impact on the identified client and the family. A variable that is rarely assessed is whether a family support program prevents family members, other than the identified client, from exhibiting dysfunctional behavior and becoming involved in the court, social service, or mental health systems. Klein, Alexander, and Parsons have conducted studies in this area.[4] However, no efforts have been made to determine if treatment obviates the transmission of family problems across generations. Measuring these variables will contribute to an understanding of the indirect, long-term benefits of working with the entire family.

Given the differences in target populations, theoretical frameworks, treatment durations and methods, intensity of service provision, and in the education and experience of the staff who deliver the services, it is difficult to compare program evaluations. In addition, programs use different evaluation instruments, which contribute to the problem of comparison. Unless consistent tools and methods are employed, it is difficult—if not impossible—to test, refine, and improve evaluation instruments and expand our knowledge.

Most family preservation programs are too young to have had longitudinal studies conducted, but we need to initiate systematic evaluations to bring credibility to these programs. "Home-based services to children . . . can scarcely expect to acquire a scientific footing or gain professional recognition as long as they remain outside the mainstream of significant scholarship being generated by such related disciplines as child development and family study."[5] Both funding sources and family preservation programs must place greater emphasis on evaluation, and must develop quantitative as well as qualitative evaluation tools.

11
Exemplary Home-Based, Family-Centered Programs

Over the past few years, many family treatment models have developed; some have promised and some have demonstrated success in working with multiproblem families. These programs vary in target populations; they serve families of preschool youngsters, adolescents, children at risk of abuse and neglect, youths with developmental disabilities, disturbed youngsters, juvenile offenders, minority youths, and others. The programs operate in urban, rural, or suburban communities, and tailor their treatment to the needs of the population.

Diverse treatment models abound, and programs vary in the intensity of service provision. Some are short-term, others are long-term; some have an individual counselor working with a family, others employ a team approach. Programs also differ in the education and experience of staff. Theoretical frameworks also differ, and most are based on one or more of the following treatment modalities: behaviorism, the client-centered approach, communication theory, modeling, social learning theory, the systems approach, strategic family therapy, structural family therapy, or the ecological approach.

This diversity of treatment approaches makes it difficult to compare programs, to discuss similarities and differences, and to recommend a comprehensive program model. Despite the inherent difficulty of comparing programs, it is important to consider the array of programs serving multiproblem families.

Based on an extensive review, a few exemplary programs are described in this chapter. Every effort has been made to present a diverse cross-section of the programs and their characteristics. The staff of each program were contacted by letter and/or by telephone at least three times, and some programs were visited. An overview of each program is provided to enable the reader to compare the various programs. A tabular appendix at the end of this chapter summarizes the key aspects of the programs. Readers are encouraged to contact the programs in which they are most interested.

Center for Family Life in Sunset Park

St. Christopher's Home
345 43rd Street

Brooklyn, New York 11232
(718) 788-3500
Sister Mary Paul, Director of Clinical Services

The Center for Family Life began in November, 1978, as part of St. Christopher's Home (which began in 1948). It is a neighborhood program that provides intensive, multidimensional, family-focused services to Sunset Park, an urban community. The program receives self-referrals as well as referrals from schools, social service agencies, courts, and from relatives of clients. The center does not accept categorical funding because it refuses to group families or individuals by presenting problems or disabilities. Services are based entirely on the needs of the individuals and on a multiple treatment approach. In developing a service plan, the program considers the individual and the family in the context of their environment, instead of allocating treatment according to a problem "category."

All of the programs use a family systems approach. The center assists individuals and families through personal counseling, helps them access normalizing opportunities, and aids them in working with social systems to obtain housing, jobs, education, and so on. Competence building, conflict resolution, and remediation are also major focuses. Assistance is provided in coordinating needed community resources. Both an individual and a team approach are used in service delivery.

The center provides clients with a number of supports, ranging from developmental to rehabilitative. In the center's experience, service based totally on remediation is ineffectual. The counselor must also take a developmental approach and work to improve the clients' quality of life. For example, a youth with behavioral problems may be successfully helped by an interactional experience in a group or activity which emphasizes developmental needs.

The center's programs include individual, group, and family counseling; family life education; an advocacy clinic; an emergency food program; a foster grandparent program; summer day camp; an infant/toddler/parent program; a big brother/big sister program; recreational activities; school-based services for children and parents (including school-age child care for youngsters five through twelve); and an employment services and job placement program. The center is very involved in working with public and private agencies to address community needs.

To be eligible for services at the center, a family must reside in the Sunset Park area of Brooklyn and have a child under eighteen. A pregnant woman residing in the Sunset Park area is also eligible. The families served are eighty percent Hispanic; other ethnic groups compose the remainder of the population. Most of the clients are from low-income, single-parent, or reconstituted families. Counseling may be in-home or at the center, whichever is more appropriate to a family's needs and to the selected methods of helping. The number of hours of direct service vary greatly from one to twenty hours per week depending on family need and the treatment modalities used. The center is open seven days a week (from 8:00 A.M. to 11:00 P.M.), and staff are available twenty-four hours a day through a telephone emergency response system. Services are not time-limited, and may last from thirty days to three years. In order to obtain feedback and recommendations for improvement, the center administers satisfaction questionnaires to participants in the child-care and day camp programs.

The center serves 662 families each year. Of these, 406 receive long-term services and 256 receive short-term services, such as emergency assistance, information, referral, and advocacy. In addition, a minimum of 300 individuals per year participate in the employment services program, and many hundreds of children and youths participate in the school-based programs. The center's fiscal year 1985–1986 budget is approximately $1 million. Eighty percent of their funding is from state and local sources, and twenty percent is private.

Sources

Janchill, Sister Mary Paul. *Guidelines to Decision-Making in Child Welfare*. New York: Human Service Workshops, 1981.

Janchill, Sister Mary Paul. Letters to the author, December 31, 1984; September 26, 1985.

McMahon, Robert J., Sister Mary Geraldine, and Sister Mary Paul. "A Progress Report: June 30, 1984." St. Christopher's Home, Brooklyn, New York, 1984. Photocopy.

Magazino, Carmine J. "Services to Children and Families at Risk of Separation." In *Child Welfare: Current Dilemmas, Future Directions*, edited by Brenda G. McGowan and William Meezan, 211–54. Itasca, Ill.: F.E. Peacock, 1983.

Children's Services Division, State of Oregon

198 Commercial Street, SE
Salem, Oregon 97310
(503) 378–3016
Marcia Allen, High Impact Services
William Showell, Intensive Family Services Program

The Children's Services Division, Oregon's child welfare agency, has been providing family therapy to its clients since 1980. As a result of a policy decision, this state agency made a commitment to family-centered services, with the goal of preventing out-of-home placement. Through involvement in Intensive Family Services (IFS), more than seventy percent of the children served have been prevented from out-of-home placement. The IFS program provides family therapy to families whose children are at risk of placement. As a result of the success of IFS, High Impact Services began in 1982. This program is preventive; it reaches families before placement is a consideration and also serves youths who are returning home from placement. Although High Impact is more of a "front-end" service than IFS, the profiles of family problems for the programs are similar.

In a recent study of 264 families in IFS and High Impact, 36 percent of the families were intact and 64 percent were single-parent. Approximately 90 percent of the families were Caucasian (compared to 95 percent of the Oregon population). The other 10 percent were black, Hispanic, Asian, and Native American families.

Both programs provide time-limited services that span a three-month period. Each family receives up to thirty-five hours of direct service, approximately two hours per week, most of which is in-home. Interventions include multiple-impact therapy, structural family therapy, strategic therapy, and communications theory. Emphasis is also placed on interfacing and working with community services. Effective collaboration between state and private agency staff is encouraged through joint training sessions. The program does not offer twenty-four-hour service. A computer follow-up system tracks whether families return to the state system. The program also tracks whether children are placed and whether there are protective service referrals subsequent to family treatment. There is no formal therapist follow-up.

IFS is directed by a family service specialist (ACSW) and has 36 family therapists. Each therapist serves 8.37 families, and each family has a primary and a secondary therapist. Cotherapy is provided when necessary. High Impact Services is directed by a family service specialist (MSW) and employs 41 therapists. Each therapist has a caseload of 11 families. Teams comprised of agency therapists and volunteers serve the families.

Ideally, family treatment staff have master's degrees in social work, psychology, or counseling, and have had one year's family counseling experience or a baccalaureate degree and a minimum of three years' continuous family counseling experience. For those holding a bachelor's degree, preference is given to individuals who majored in social work, psychology, or counseling.

Comprehensive descriptions and program evaluations of IFS and High Impact Services are available. The treatment model used by both programs is discussed in depth; it is divided into three stages: assessment, treatment, and termination. The model is most effective when cotherapists are involved and when a multiple-impact strategy of treatment is used, such that multiple therapists spend almost an entire day doing therapy.

High Impact Services shares a budget with the other Children's Services Division programs. No new funds were used to begin this program; staff were carved out of existing agency personnel. Family workers carry smaller caseloads for a shorter period of time, but have about the same number of clients as other counselors in the Children's Services Division.

Eleven of the sixteen IFS programs are contracted out to private agencies or individuals, and five are staffed by Children's Services Division employees. The fiscal year 1985–1986 budget for the eleven contracted programs is $1,033,187, which is divided among twenty-two supervisors, family therapists, and clerical and administrative staff.

The IFS budget was developed by shifting money from the foster care to the IFS budget. It was projected that by keeping high-risk children at home, a foster care budget offset would pay for IFS. The money has two sources: Title IV–B and state general funds.

IFS serves 1,188 families per year (33 families per therapist); the average cost of services is $1,131.85 per family. High Impact Services serves 1,804 families per year (44 families per therapist); its cost per family has not been calculated.

Sources

Allen, Marcia. Letters to the author, August 9, 1985; September 4, 1985.
Allen, Marcia. "Report on CSD High Impact Services." Children's Services Division, Salem, Oregon. April 8, 1985. Photocopy.
Hartley, Roland. "High Impact Services Implementation Handbook." Children's Services Division, Salem, Oregon. November 7, 1983. Photocopy.
Showell, William H. "1983–85 Biennial Report of CSD's Intensive Family Services." Children's Services Division, Salem, Oregon. April 5, 1985. Photocopy.
Showell, William H. "Report of CSD Intensive Family Services." Children's Services Division, Salem, Oregon. February 3, 1983. Photocopy.
Showell, William, Marcia Allen, and Ted Keys. "The Oregon Intensive Family Services (IFS) and High Impact Family Treatment Model." Children's Services Division, Salem, Oregon. December 6, 1983. Photocopy.

Head Start

20 Union Street
Brockton, Massachusetts 02401
(617) 587–1716
Ruth Taylor, Social Services Coordinator

Head Start programs began in 1965. They are the forerunner of family preservation programs, yet their impact and importance is often overlooked. Head Start programs are intended to break the cycle of poverty by providing comprehensive services to preschool children from low-income families. Head

Start also serves handicapped children, who now make up 11.9 percent of children in the program.

All Head Start programs have four components: education, health, parent involvement, and social services. An educational program is tailored to meet the needs of each child and to reflect the cultural and ethnic background of the community served. (For example, if a community is Hispanic, Spanish-speaking staff are hired.) Head Start programs have a low teacher/child ratio, which enables teachers to work closely with children. In addition, there is a strong emphasis on early recognition of health problems. Each child receives thorough medical, dental, psychological, and nutritional care. Parental involvement is also strongly encouraged, because Head Start recognizes that parents know more about their children than anyone else and that they have the most impact on their children's development. Parents can become involved in Head Start in four ways: decision making about program operation; working in the classroom as paid employees, volunteers, or observers; participating in parent activities initiated by other Head Start parents; and working with their children in their homes, with assistance from Head Start staff. Head Start helps parents gain access to needed social services.

Head Start programs exist throughout the United States, but the specific program highlighted here demonstrates how Head Start programs operate and how they affect participants. Head Start strongly emphasizes empowering parents by encouraging them to participate in their children's lives and to enhance their own lives.

Brockton has the second-largest Head Start program in Massachusetts. It began in 1965, and presently has twenty-two centers located in nine communities; these centers serve urban, suburban, and rural areas. The centers operate all year, except for the summer, when only the Brockton center is open to serve twenty-seven high-risk, special needs children. Families in the summer program receive twenty hours per week of direct service.

Brockton Head Start receives referrals from public schools, private agencies, pediatricians, and pediatric hospitals, as well as self-referrals. The program serves 530 youngsters, 50 of whom are in a home-based program. Youths in the home-based program attend classes at the center only three times per month; their parents have chosen to have their children receive services in their homes rather than in regular classes. These families receive 3.25 hours per week of direct service. During the school year, the center-based program operates for four hours a day, four days a week. On one weekday, teachers do classroom planning and make home visits. Home visitors educate the children and parent(s) and offer social services on a weekly basis. Families in the center-based program receive sixteen hours per week of direct service. Head Start is not available twenty-four hours a day.

The youths served are from three to four years of age. Ninety percent are from single-parent households. Most of the families meet poverty guidelines; however, ten percent have special needs and are above poverty guidelines. Families vary in ethnic and cultural background. Brockton Head Start aims to empower families and help them build networks that will support them when the program ends.

Parents play an important role in Head Start. Each center has a parent group that meets once a month. A representative and an alternate are elected to a policy council, which sets policy and makes decisions for the entire program. Parents also participate as volunteers; they may be involved in any part of the program, such as the classroom, kitchen, or clerical office. A weekly parent support group is another important aspect of Head Start. Two types of groups operate: one lasts for eight to ten sessions, the other is twenty sessions. Each center decides if and when parent support groups will be held.

The home-based program at Head Start has five home visitors, each with a caseload of ten families. The home visitor assesses and addresses the psychological, health, educational, and social service needs of a youngster. Each child is given a developmental test, and the home visitor designs a program with the parent(s) to help meet a youngster's developmental needs. The home visitor also helps parent(s) access community resources.

At Brockton Head Start, a director, an assistant director, a special needs coordinator, and the administrative staff oversee four components of the program: social services, health, education, and parent involvement. The social services component has a coordinator, two family service specialists, and twelve family workers. The health component is made up of two nurses, a health unit manager, and a nursing consultant. The educational component has an educational director, four educational specialists, and sixty teaching staff. In the parent involvement component, a parent volunteer coordinator and two volunteers canvas for community and parent volunteers.

Each classroom has two teachers, a special needs aide (as necessary), a family worker, and a health worker. Program support staff consist of an educational specialist, who supervises five to six classrooms, and a family service specialist, who supervises the family workers in ten classrooms.

The family worker does all of the recruitment and enrollment for his or her own classrooms by meeting with community agencies and public schools to get referrals. Each family worker is assigned to two classrooms and has a caseload of forty families. The family worker and the parent(s) develop a family service plan to assess whether the family needs community resources; the family worker also provides information and makes referrals, as necessary. He or she structures the parent group, and helps the group elect representatives and understand group decision making. The family workers also support teaching staff dealing with family issues. The family workers at Brockton Head Start are all paraprofessionals whose children had participated in the program.

Brockton Head Start's fiscal year 1985–1986 budget is $1,724,178. Eighty percent of this amount comes from federal funding and twenty percent represents local support, including volunteer time and donated classroom space. Services are provided for one to two years. The average cost per family for the center-based program is $2,598, $2,106 for the home-based program.

Sources

Curry-Rood, Leah, Larry A. Rood, and Sylvia E. Carter. *Head Start Parent Handbook Revised Edition*. Mt. Rainer, Md: Gryphon House, 1978.
Taylor, Ruth. Interview with the author. Brockton, Massachusetts, July 9, 1985.

Home and Community Treatment

Mendota Mental Health Institute
301 Troy Drive
Madison, Wisconsin 53704
(608) 244–2411
Mary Ann Fahl, Unit Chief

The Home and Community Treatment Program (HCT) began in 1969, when the Children's Treatment Center (established in 1860) was an autonomous agency; in 1973 the facility was subsumed by Mendota State Hospital and changed its name to Mendota Mental Health Institute. HCT is one of the oldest family preservation programs; a number of other programs are based on it. HCT serves Dane County, which consists of urban, suburban, and some rural areas, and provides training and consultation throughout the state. HCT serves three- to ten-year-old children diagnosed as having emotional or behavioral problems.

Referrals, channeled through the Community Mental Health Board of Dane County, are made by private practitioners, clinics, schools, or social service agencies. The board insures that families referred have failed to respond to less intensive treatment. Admission criteria are: the family must reside in Dane County; all the people living in the household must agree to try a new approach; a child must demonstrate functional weaknesses or excesses in social, cognitive, or emotional development; the problem must be in the parent-child interaction; the adults must agree to let outsiders into their home; the adults must allocate time to work with their children; the adults must follow other adults' directions and recognize that, as parents, they have a strong influence on their children.

Ninety percent of the families served are Caucasian; forty percent are intact families, sixty percent are single parent, and most are working class. HCT takes a systems approach, and treatment is based on social learning theory and behavior management. Parents in the program examine their own behavior as well as their child's, and learn what they can reasonably expect from their child as well as how to affect the child's behavior. Treatment entails individualized child management programs, which are implemented by the child's family and teachers, with staff guidance. Play therapy, individual therapy, and marital therapy are available as needed.

Treatment begins with a negotiated written agreement that outlines the roles and responsibilities of the family and the treatment team members for a specified period of time. Each individual signs this first agreement, which includes detailed procedures for home and school observations. The agreement also sets out the interactional difficulties in the family and takes baseline measures of identified child and adult target behaviors. After a two- to four-week observation and diagnostic period, the treatment team gives the family feedback about their specific strengths and weaknesses in adult-child interaction.

Treatment begins by giving the parents didactic training in the principles of behavior management; this is followed by role playing and modeling, in which staff demonstrate techniques and prompt family members and/or teachers in their use. Staff then provide immediate feedback. Case planning is guided by behavioral data, which is assessed every one to two months.

Initially, a family is seen more often in the office than in the home. They learn skills of child management in the office, but as time goes on, a family is seen more often in the home, so that they can transfer skills from the office to the home. Contact with the family and school is most intensive at the beginning of treatment (four to twelve or more hours in three to eight visits per week) and typically diminishes to an average of two to four hours per week. The staff of the program are not available twenty-four hours a day; community agencies provide this service. The average length of treatment is fifteen months. Although there is no routine follow-up, a family is encouraged to contact staff if it has questions or problems.

The staff is transdisciplinary, and consists of a nurse, psychologist, social worker, and occupational therapist (who directs the program). No particular level of training is required; experience and the willingness to take risks are valued more than degrees. Staff work in teams that carry a caseload of six families. One team member becomes the case manager and assumes responsibility for service coordination and case documentation.

HCT serves twelve families per year. The program receives state money, contributions from private insurance, and client fees. The fiscal year 1985–1986 budget was approximately $150,000 and represents 0.7 percent of the total agency budget. The annual average cost of service is $11,250 per family, compared to an average inpatient annual cost of $86,000 ($236.00 per day).

Sources

Cautley, Patricia W. *The Home and Community Treatment Process: Helping Families Change.* Madison, Wisc.: Home and Community Treatment, Mendota Mental Health Institute, November, 1979.

Cautley, Patricia W., and Mary Beth Plane. *Facilitating Family Change: A Look at Four Agencies Working Intensively with Families.* Madison, Wisc.: Wisconsin Department of Health and Social Services, Division of Community Services, May, 1983.

Fahl, Mary Ann. "Shaping Parent-Child Interactions: A Behavioral Model in a Family Context." In *Treating Families in the Home: An Alternative to Placement,* edited by Marvin Bryce and June C. Lloyd, 165–79. Springfield, Ill.: Charles C Thomas, 1981.

Fahl, Mary Ann, and Donna Morrissey. "The Mendota Model: Home-Community Treatment." In *Home-Based Services for Children and Families: Policy, Practice and Research,* edited by Sheila Maybanks and Marvin Bryce, 225–36. Springfield, Ill.: Charles C Thomas, 1979.

Fahl, Mary Ann. Letter to the author, August 28, 1985.

Fahl, Mary Ann. Telephone conversation with the author, July 3, 1985.

Homebuilders, Behavioral Sciences Institute

1717 South 341st Place, Suite B
Federal Way, Washington 98003
(206) 927–1550
Jill Kinney and David Haapala, Codirectors

Homebuilders began in October, 1974, as part of Catholic Community Services of Tacoma, Washington. In 1981, the Behavioral Sciences Institute was created; Homebuilders is a division of this agency. The program provides intensive, home-based family crisis intervention and education. Its goals are to prevent out-of-home placement of family members and to increase family integrity through immediate intervention that defuses the crisis, stabilizes the family, and teaches family members new problem-resolution skills, so that they can avoid future crises. Homebuilders intervenes when a family has reached a crisis and all other less intensive resources are exhausted. Staff find that family members are more willing to experiment with new ideas and behaviors when their old methods of solving problems no longer work. The presence of Homebuilder staff at a stressful time creates a bond between the therapist and the family, and thus increases the likelihood of successful treatment.

Homebuilders serves urban, suburban, and rural areas. Programs operate in King County (Seattle), Pierce County (Tacoma), Snohomish County, and Spokane County. Half of the children served are female and half are male. The other characteristics of the families served are given in Table 11–1.

Table 11–1
Characteristics of Families Served by Homebuilders

Characteristic	Percentage
Annual Income	
$0–5,000	19
$5,000–$10,000	26
$10,000–$20,000	27
$20,000–$30,000	19
$30,000 +	8
Family Composition	
Single Parent	47
Step-Parent and Blended families	32
Two Natural Parents	21
Family Size	
Two Members	11
Three Members	22
Four Members	31
Five Members	14
Six Members	11
Over Six Members	6
Racial Group	
Caucasian	83
Black	11
Indian	4
Asian	1
Native American	1
Problems	
Family Violence	33
Adult Mental Health Problems	14
Parent-Child Conflict	78
Child Abuse and Neglect	48

Clients are referred from the Washington State Department of Social and Health Services. To be accepted by the program, the referral source and the family must agree that, without Homebuilders' intervention, a child will have to be placed.

Therapists work with families over a four- to six-week period, although treatment is targeted to last four weeks. Therapists spend as much time as necessary with families and are personally available twenty-four hours a day. It is estimated that therapists often put in nearly a year's worth of outpatient counseling in one month. Although the number of hours that therapists work with families varies greatly, the average number of hours per family per week is distributed as follows:

Face to face contact	9.8
Telephone contact with a family	1.0
Collateral contact (case consultation with other service providers, etc.)	0.7
Travel	2.7
Other (paperwork)	2.7
Total	16.9 hours

Each therapist's caseload is two families, to insure comprehensive, individualized service. Typically, one therapist works with each family, but additional therapists may be used as necessary.

Homebuilders takes a psychoeducational approach. Primary treatment modalities include client-centered therapy, behavior and emotion management, behavioral rehearsal, communication skills building, rational emotive therapy, crisis intervention, a territorial approach to human relations (an understanding of how people share physical and psychological space), and concrete services (such as provision of food or transportation). Therapists have three major roles: observer, listener, and teacher. Homebuilders works with each family during a crisis period and then, when requested and feasible, refers the family to appropriate community resources. The therapist may help the family make the transition to a community resource, and will sometimes accompany family members to the first session.

Once Homebuilders has terminated its relationship with families, it is unusual for them to be referred to the agency again. Rereferral has happened in less than five percent of the cases; generally referrals are for another child or occur when parents have remarried. After termination, each family completes a client satisfaction survey. Therapists are available for emergency follow-up telephone calls and occasional sessions.

The staff consists of two coexecutive directors, an associate director, and the equivalent of twenty-three full-time therapists. All the staff currently possess master's degrees; however, this is not a requirement. Homebuilders seeks the following characteristics in staff: a strong Rogerian background (that is, a person who understands Rogerian theory and can listen actively and nonjudgmentally, especially in a crisis); a background in behavioral therapy and social learning theory; an understanding of rational emotive therapy; experience with values clarification; and a territorial approach to human relations.

Between 1975 and 1984, Homebuilders served 1,921 families. Three months after termination, 94 percent of the children were still in their homes. Homebuilders serves 359 families per year (481 children targeted for placement). Twelve-month follow-up information, available after September, 1982, shows that 90 percent of the children targeted for residential care avoided placement. The average cost of serving each child in danger of placement is $1,980. Homebuilders has documented that it is far more economical than out-of-home placement.

Homebuilders' budget for fiscal year 1985–1986 is $1,069,000 in contracted service through the Washington State Department of Social and Health Services. The Behavioral Sciences Institute also operates a research division and a training division.

Homebuilders has been replicated in a number of states. The agency's experience in designing a home-based family preservation program merits consideration. The Training Division in the Behavioral Sciences Institute offers a wide range of training and consultation services. However, the printed materials, training, and consultation provided by Homebuilders is expensive.

Sources

Haapala, David. Letters to the author, July 23, 1985; September 10, 1985.

Haapala, David. Telephone conversation with the author, June 17, 1985.

Haapala, David. "Perceived Helpfulness, Attributed Critical Incident Responsibility, and a Discrimination of Home Based Family Therapy Treatment Outcomes: Homebuilders Model." Catholic Community Services, Tacoma, Washington, and Behavioral Sciences Institute, Federal Way, Washington. November, 1983. Photocopy.

Haapala, David, and Jill Kinney. "Homebuilders' Approach to the Training of In-Home Therapists." In *Home-Based Services for Children and Families: Policy, Practice and Research,* edited by Sheila Maybanks and Marvin Bryce, 248–59, Springfield, Ill.: Charles C Thomas, 1979.

"Home Therapy Program Keeps Kids Out of Institutions and Foster Homes." *Behavior Today* 13, no. 11 (March 22, 1982):5–7.

Horn, Jack C. "House-calls for Families in Crisis." *Psychology Today* 10, no. 7 (Dec. 1976):113–14.

Kinney, Jill. "Brief Home-Based Intervention Is Effective." *Permanency Report* 2, no. 2 (spring 1984):2.

Kinney, Jill. "Homebuilders: An In-Home Crisis Intervention Program." *Children Today* 7, no. 1 (Jan.–Feb. 1978):15–17, 35.

Kinney, Jill, and David Haapala. "Behavioral Sciences Institute Overview of the Homebuilder Program." Behavioral Sciences Institute, Federal Way, Washington. [no date]. Photocopy.

Kinney, Jill, and David Haapala. "Prevention of Violence in In-Home Family Crisis Intervention." [no date]. Photocopy.

Kinney, Jill, David Haapala, and Joan Elizabeth Gast. "Assessment of Families in Crisis." In *Treating Families in the Home: An Alternative to Placement,* edited by Marvin Bryce and June C. Lloyd, 50–67. Springfield, Ill.: Charles C Thomas, 1981.

Kinney, Jill McCleave, Barbara Madsen, Thomas Fleming, and David Haapala. "Homebuilders: Keeping Families Together." *Journal of Consulting and Clinical Psychology* 45, no. 4 (Aug. 1977):667–73.

"Live-In Therapy." *Human Behavior* 5, no. 10 (Oct. 1976):39.

Slater, Edward P., and William R. Harris. "Therapy at Home." *Practice Digest* 1, no. 1 (June 1978):20–21.

Family Based Service

Crittenton Family Support Center, Youth Service, Inc.
6325 Burbridge Street
Philadelphia, Pennsylvania 19144
(215) 848–6200
Gail Purdie, Director

Family Based Service of Youth Service, Inc., established in January, 1974, provides intensive, long-term, home-based services to families in Philadelphia. The program's goals are to prevent placement and to reunite families if placement has already occurred. All referrals come from the Philadelphia County Children and Youth Agency when it becomes concerned about emotional or physical abuse or neglect. Approximately half of the families served are court-involved. Seventy-four percent are black, twenty percent are Caucasian, four percent are Hispanic, and two percent are interracial. One-third of the families have an adult male in the home. All of the families are on public assistance, Supplementary Security Income (public assistance to the aged, blind, and disabled), or Social Security. Most are isolated and have few positive relationships or supports.

Before a family is accepted in the program, a two-visit intake study is conducted to explain the services and assess a family's willingness to participate. Parent(s) sign a contract that commits them to be available at specific times to work on mutually agreed goals.

Case assignments are made by the intake worker and the supervisor based on the family's needs and staff availability. A family is assigned to a team, or a social worker, or a family care worker; if a family requires intensive services, a team is assigned. Clear, specific criteria for case assignment determine whether an individual or a team approach is used.

Workers provide both concrete and psychological services. The methods of service are family therapy, a systems approach, a developmental approach, concrete services, and linking the family with community resources. Staff are available twenty-four hours a day, seven days a week. The specific services provided include individual, couple, family, extended family, and crisis intervention counseling; hands-on assistance, such as life skills education (for example, budgeting, grooming, hygiene), home management and scheduling, parenting, sex education, and family planning; linkages with community resources (mostly medical, court, and educational/vocational resources; housing; utility companies; and public assistance); parent support groups; and an emergency food bank.

A family's immediate needs take precedence over discussing their psychological problems. Families have many crises, for example, their utilities may have been cut off, they may not have anywhere to live, or they may not have enough food. Although three social workers on staff are trained in structural family therapy, this type of treatment is modified, because families are not highly verbal or insightful.

The program views the mother as the primary client because changes in family dynamics and behavior happen through her. Extensive efforts are made to build the mother's self-esteem by treating her as an adult, listening to her opinions, reinforcing her strengths, and helping her learn how to cope more effectively with problems. The program has found that if staff fail to focus initially on the mother's needs, she will be unable to work toward effectively meeting her children's needs.

Within the first three months of treatment, and every six months thereafter, a study of the adequacy of housing is conducted. Through money from United Way, a handyman repairs homes. In addition, money is available to help families in crises, for example, to pay utility bills or purchase furniture. Staff recognize that it is important for families to contribute to purchases, if possible; staff actively discourage financial dependency on the program.

A primary focus of the program is on helping families utilize community resources. Workers prepare families for using these resources, and accompany them until family members feel comfortable enough to access services on their own.

The program staff consist of a director (MSW), six social workers (MSWs), and four family care workers (BSWs, BAs, and those with Associate's degrees). Each social worker has a caseload of ten to twelve families. A social worker's responsibilities include counseling, case management, linking families with community resources, and supervising family care workers.

Social work services comprise one to three hours per week of home-based services. Each family care worker has a caseload of six families, and works directly with a family for three to seven hours per week. The family care worker concentrates on empowering parents by assisting in the day-to-day management of the children and the household. The family care worker and the social worker communicate frequently by telephone, notes, and informal conversations. They meet weekly for case planning and supervision. The program does not offer formal follow-up services.

The fiscal year 1985–1986 budget is $423,524. Sixty-six percent comes from local support; thirty-four percent is private. The program serves 125 families per year. The frequency of direct services ranges from two to ten hours per week, depending on the family's need. The average length of service is twenty months. The average cost of services per family is from $6,000 to $6,500 per year.

Sources

Purdie, Gail. Letter to the author, August 28, 1985.

Purdie, Gail. Telephone conversation with the author, Philadelphia, Pennsylvania, June 28, 1985.

Purdie, Gail, and Theodore Levine. "Family Based Care: A Ten Year Review of Service Delivery and Outcomes and Its Impact on the Program." Paper presented at the Child Welfare League of America Conference, Washington, D.C., June, 1984.

In-Home Family Counseling/Support Services

Iowa Children's & Family Services
1101 Walnut
Des Moines, Iowa 50309
(515) 288–1981
Linda M. Ross, Director, Department of Family Counseling

The parent agency of In-Home Family Counseling/Support Services began in 1888. The home-based, family-centered program began in June, 1977, and currently serves forty counties in Iowa through six offices. Families are referred by the Department of Human Services, Juvenile Court, schools, or employee assistance programs; they may also refer themselves. A comprehensive range of in-home family services is offered, including counseling (individual, marital, and family), teaching, role modeling, family advocacy, and assistance in accessing community resources. Structural family therapy and an ecological approach are utilized.

The program serves urban, suburban, and rural areas; many of the clients are socially isolated rural families. Clients are predominantly Caucasian, most are low income, and fifty percent are single-parent families. Each counselor has a caseload of four to seven families; supervisory staff carry one to four cases. An in-home family counselor is assigned to each family. Families receive approximately six hours of service per week; three of these hours are in-home. Staff are available twenty-four hours a day to respond to crises. The services are time-limited, and last approximately six months. A follow-up visit is made six months after termination.

The staff consist of a director (MPA and MS), four program supervisors (two MAs, one BA, and one MSW candidate), one assistant program supervisor (BSW, MSW candidate) and twenty-five in-home family counselors (sixteen BAs, BSs, and BSWs; three MSWs; and six MAs and MSs). In order to qualify for a position, a bachelor's degree (preferably in social work or a related field) and family service experience are preferred.

In-Home Family Counseling/Support Services has documented its impressive success in preventing placement. In fiscal year 1983–1984, the program served 297 families, at a cost of approximately $2,737 per family. The program's fiscal year 1985–1986 budget is $883,000, which represents twenty-five percent of the agency's total budget. Ninety percent of the program's money comes from the state; ten percent from private sources.

Sources

Ross, Linda. Telephone conversation with the author, May 31, 1985.

Ross, Linda. Letters to the author, March 29, 1985; July 19, 1985.

Stephens, Douglas. "In-Home Family Support Services: An Ecological Systems Approach." In *Home-Based Services for Children and Families: Policy, Practice, and Research,* edited by Sheila Maybanks and Marvin Bryce, 283–95. Springfield, Ill.: Charles C Thomas, 1979.

Stephens, Douglas B., and Kay F. Busch. "Strategies of Ecological Change with Families." In *Treating Families in the Home: An Alternative to Placement,* edited by Marvin Bryce and June C. Lloyd, 152–64. Springfield, Ill.: Charles C Thomas, 1981.

Lower East Side Family Union

84 Stanton Street
New York, New York 10002
(212) 260–0040
Alfred B. Herbert, Jr., Executive Director

The Lower East Side Family Union (LESFU) began in 1972 in response to a 1971 report published by the Citizen's Committee for Children, an advocacy group. The report noted the need to fund services to keep families together to avoid foster care placement. LESFU evolved from the collaboration of the executive directors of five settlement houses and three agencies on the Lower East Side. This is one of the poorest sections of New York City and has a large ethnic population. Hispanics make up forty-five percent of the clients, Chinese thirty-five percent, and blacks and Caucasians twenty percent. Ninety percent of the families are on public assistance. They have a multitude of social and environmental problems.

LESFU was established in response to a fragmented, poorly coordinated, often conflictual service system. The agency serves families in danger of dissolution. To qualify for services, families must reside on the Lower East Side and have at least one child under eighteen. Most referrals come from public child welfare agencies; however, families are also referred by courts, schools, police, social service agencies, the clergy, and families who have been clients of LESFU. The agency aims to prevent foster care by empowering families and helping parents learn to care for their children.

LESFU has three major goals: to help families locate and obtain needed services through a case management approach; to coordinate, integrate, and monitor the services provided; and to offer direct services such as homemaking, counseling, and advocacy. LESFU's treatment model has seven stages: a prework agreement, a work agreement, goal setting, convening, contracting, monitoring, and follow-up. The agency works with each family to establish and prioritize its needs and develop strategies to address the identified problems. An initial assessment of one to five sessions is followed by a conference in which a social work associate and family members meet with agency representatives, who agree to provide the family with services. A contract delineating responsibilities is signed by everyone. The social work associate monitors the services and insures that the contract is upheld by all parties.

LESFU services are provided by five teams. Each team is directed by a social worker who has earned a master's degree. The outreach team is responsible for finding cases and conducting intake for all geographic areas. This team consists of the outreach coordinator and three outreach workers. The other four teams are each responsible for a specific geographic area. They are composed of team leaders, social work associates, (BS or BSW degree required), family workers (life experience required), and secretaries. One of the five teams offers specialized services to families whose children are at risk of abuse or neglect. This team receives most of its referrals from Special Services for Children, the city's social service agency. A team leader supervises and manages each team. The social work associate carries fifteen cases, and works with each family to ensure that it makes full use of community resources. The family worker carries eight cases, and provides child care, homemaking, budget management, and help with accessing services, as necessary. He or she teaches family members how to help themselves.

LESFU has forty staff, only four of which are administrative; the majority provide direct service. Staff come from the same ethnic backgrounds as those in the neighborhoods they serve; most staff live on the Lower East Side and are bilingual. The staff's life experiences may be similar to those of LESFU clients. Although staff work as a team, each team member provides a specific service; the whole team rarely visits a family's home. Each family receives twenty hours a week of direct service. Staff are not yet available on a twenty-four-hour basis, but a system is being instituted. (It is difficult to find a beeper system that is compatible with the languages of clients—Spanish and Chinese—and that will operate without push-button telephones.)

A comprehensive program evaluation conducted by Columbia University over a three-year period has just been released. Researchers interviewed LESFU clients and staff and based their findings on a management system in place at the agency. The evaluation thoroughly describes the clients served and stresses the strong negative impact of the physical environment. The neighborhoods suffer from inadequate housing, housing shortages, and residents with severe drug problems. The report lists what clients consider to be their major problems and indicates whether or not these problems were resolved through involvement with LESFU. A substudy examines the rate of resolution of client problems, the amount of time spent on each problem, how far families advanced through the seven stages of LESFU, and which cases were the most difficult for staff to resolve. Results from this substudy will be compared to the data from client interviews in order to validate the findings of each of the studies.

LESFU's fiscal year 1985–1986 budget is just over $1 million. City and state money account for eighty-seven percent of the budget; the remainder is from foundations. LESFU serves 350 families per year. The average length of service is eighteen months. The average cost of service per family is $2,250.

Sources

Beck, Bertram. M. *The Lower East Side Family Union: A Social Invention.* New York: Foundation for Child Development. March, 1979.

Bush, Sherida. "A Family-Help Program That Really Works." *Psychology Today* 12 (May 1977):48, 50, 84, 88.

Dunu, Marylee. "The Lower East Side Family Union: Assuring Community Services for Minority Families." In *Home-Based Services for Children and Families: Policy, Practice, and Research,* edited by Sheila Maybanks and Marvin Bryce, 211–24. Springfield, Ill.: Charles C Thomas, 1979.

"Family Union Keeps Families Together." *Practice Digest* 1, no. 1 (June 1979):22–23.

Fanshel, David. "Early Findings from a Study of Families at Risk Known to the Lower East Side Family Union." Paper presented at the 10th Anniversary Conference of the Lower East Side Family Union, New York City, May 16, 1985. Photocopy.

Herbert, Alfred and staff. Interview with the author. New York City, August 2, 1985.

Marsters, Paul, Stephen J. Finch, David Fanshel, and Jaime Alvelo. "First Analyses of Lower East Side Family Union's Management Information System." New York City [1985]. Photocopy.

"New York City Agency Keeps Families Together," *Children's Defense Fund (CDF) Report* 2, no. 9 (Nov. 1980).

Weissman, Harold H. *Integrating Services for Troubled Families: Dilemmas of Program Design and Implementation.* San Francisco: Jossey-Bass, 1978.

Maine Home-Based Services

Maine Department of Mental Health and Mental Retardation
Office of Children's Services
411 State Office Building, Station 40
Augusta, Maine 04333
(207) 289–4250
Edward C. Hinckley, Director of Children's Services

Maine's first home-based family preservation program began in 1980, and nine programs currently serve urban, suburban, and rural areas. Families with children up to twenty years of age are served; children from nine to fifteen are a priority.

The Maine Department of Mental Health and Mental Retardation funds all of the family preservation programs. Seven programs receive joint funding from one or more of the following agencies: the Department of Corrections, the Department of Human Services, and the Department of Educational and Cultural Services. Maine Home-Based Services has become a highly recognized, well-established model for other states. The program is based on Homebuilders, of the Behavioral Sciences Institute in Tacoma, Washington (which has copyrighted the name, Homebuilders), and on the Iowa Children's and Family Services in Des Moines, Iowa. The Maine programs have three primary objectives: to preserve a family, by keeping a child in the home; to diffuse the crisis that caused the referral; and to link a family with continuing community support, as necessary.

The Maine programs have five core components. First, the service is time-limited, extending over a nine- to twelve-week period. The time limit on treatment makes both the family and the counselor aware of time constraints and induces more rapid change. Also, the in-home service is problem-specific: it only intervenes when a crisis makes the removal of a child imminent. Third, the service is family-oriented; that is, it involves the entire family and significant others. Fourth, the service is provided in the home, during hours that are convenient for the family. The service is delivered by teams; one team serves three to six families at a time. Each team provides three to six hours of direct service, and six to eleven hours of collateral services per week to each family. Counselors are on call twenty-four hours a day.

A unique and crucial aspect of each program is the multiagency, regional advisory committee, which is composed of representatives from all the child and family agencies or resources in the program's geographic area. Each program has a committee which meets almost monthly, to provide a forum for networking; to help members understand referral criteria and procedures and obviate inappropriate referrals; to promote a clear understanding among members of each other's roles and responsibilities; and to establish an esprit de corps among members that will ensure cooperative efforts in assisting multiproblem families. If there are problems in effecting a referral or linkage to a community resource, local service providers on the advisory committee are invested in the program by virtue of their committee membership, and accessible for problem resolution. The advisory committee is intrinsic to the success of each family preservation program.

Program staff use a short-term, goal-oriented, integrated systemic approach. They educate, act as role models, advocate for clients, and help them link with formal and informal community resources. Each program employs its own treatment modalities.

No particular credentials are required of staff; experience is valued more than degrees. All of the programs greatly emphasize training and clinical supervision. The programs offer excellent training opportunities, which include intensive annual training sessions and monthly meetings that provide mutual support and education for staff.

A two-team, home-based service, with a half-time director, four full-time counselors, a full-time secretary/bookkeeper, and clinical supervision once a week costs between $130,000 and $150,000 annually. Two teams serve twenty-four to forty-eight cases each year. The cost per family is from $3,125 to $6,250. This is a considerable savings compared to out-of-home placement in Maine, which costs $4,500 for foster care; between $10,000 and $12,000 for group homes; $15,000 for emergency shelters; $20,000 for state institutions; and from $25,000 to $30,000 for private treatment centers.

All of the programs offer limited follow-up; staff contact families at six- and twelve-month intervals to assess family functioning. To date, the overall success rate of the programs is seventy percent. The intervention is considered a success if a child is still in the home, and has not been placed in substitute care, treatment, or correctional facilities.

Sources

Drach, Kerry M. "Mental Health Program Intervention Through Networking." August 31, 1984. Photocopy.

Fuller, Francis. "Homebuilder Training." Machias, Maine, Families United [no date]. Photocopy.

Hinckley, Edward C. "Homebuilders: Home Treatment for Families." Paper presented at the Community Program Innovations conference, Community-Based Programming: Approaches for Increasing Autonomy, Empowerment and Independence, Boston, June, 1984.

Hinckley, Edward C. "Homebuilders: The Maine Experience." *Children Today* 13, no. 5 (Sept.–Oct. 1984): 14–17, 36.

Hinckley, Edward. Interview with the author. Danvers, Massachusetts, August 30, 1985.

Hinckley, Edward C. "How to Develop Coordinated, Interdepartmental Public-Agency Support for Home-Based Services: The Maine Experience." *Permanency Report* 3, no. 1 (winter 1985):2.

"Home Treatment for Families." *Practice Digest* 6, no. 2 (autumn 1983):19–21.

Parents and Children Together (PACT)
Wayne State University

45 Knapp Building
71 East Ferry
Detroit, Michigan 48202
(313) 577–3519
Dorothy Kispert, Project Director
Mary Jane S. Van Meter, Principal Investigator

PACT, established in June, 1977, is affiliated with the Department of Family and Consumer Resources at Wayne State University. Its goal is to prevent or shorten foster care placement or facilitate permanent placement. Referrals are made by Children and Youth Services of Michigan/Wayne County Department of Social Services; all of the referrals are substantiated cases of child abuse or neglect. The program gives short-term treatment, and serves multiproblem families in Wayne County, an urban area. The majority of families are single parent and on public assistance. Seventy-five percent are black.

Through in-home counseling, counselors, in partnership with families, help with realistic goal-setting and contracting. Major services include in-home counseling and education, parent groups, transportation, donations, home repairs, and a twenty-four-hour emergency telephone service. Parent groups are available for PACT parents; four to six groups run concurrently on a ten-week schedule. Groups are small, and transportation and child care are provided. Through parent groups, parenting skills are improved and self-esteem is enhanced. An ongoing group is led by women who have been through the PACT program (peer counselors). In addition, transportation is provided to help families with household moves. Money is set aside for emergency home repairs, and donations such as beds, dressers, and stoves are obtained for families. The program gives priority to families whose children are about to return from foster care, and to families whose children can be prevented from placement as a result of assistance.

PACT emphasizes goal-setting; behavior management; a strong, trusting counselor-family relationship; social learning theory; role modeling; education; creating and strengthening supportive systems for families through an ecological approach; and effective coordination of services through family support and advocacy. The counselor-family relationship is primary; the family views the counselor as a friend and receives very individualized services.

PACT trains graduate students from the Department of Family and Consumer Resources at Wayne State University who plan to work in human services. Students earn twelve graduate credit hours during a year's internship, and, under supervision, maintain a caseload of eight families. Counselors work with families individually; they provide two hours per week of direct service and offer additional support services to each family. Each counselor is paid for a twenty-nine-hour work week. Seventy-five percent of all service hours are in a family's home. The program offers no formal follow-up services for families. Research and evaluation are conducted by a principal investigator.

The PACT staff includes a principal investigator (PhD); a project director (MA); a coordinator of in-home counseling (MSW), who supervises one intake and referral worker (BA), three counselor supervisors (MAs or MSWs), and twenty-two counselors; a parent group coordinator (ACSW), who supervises two parent group workers (MSW), who, in turn, supervise three child care workers and three peer counselors; and a coordinator of transportation, who supervises a driver and handyman. PACT seeks individuals with MSW degrees for the positions of parent group coordinator, parent group workers, and coordinator of in-home counseling. Counselor supervisors need to have MSW degrees or master's degrees in human development and family relations.

In 1983–1984, 318 families (1,049 children) were served. Ninety-three percent of the children who were at high risk of placement remained in their homes; thirty-three percent of the children in foster care at the beginning of the service returned home. Six percent of the children received permanency planning services.

PACT is funded solely by Children and Youth Services of the Michigan/Wayne County Department of Social Services. The program's fiscal year 1985–1986 budget is $610,000. The average length of service for each family is 8.1 months, and the average cost per family is $1,900.

Sources

Cabral, R.J., and E.D. Callard. "A Home-Based Program to Serve High-Risk, Families." *Journal of Home Economics* (fall 1982):14–19.

Giblin, P.T., and E.D. Callard. "Issues in Evaluation of Action Research: A Social Service Model." *Social Work Research and Abstracts* 16, no. 4 (winter 1980):3–12.

Morin, Patricia. "The Extended Family Model: Increasing Service Effectiveness." In *Treating Families in the Home: An Alternative to Placement,* edited by Marvin Bryce and June C. Lloyd, 135–51. Springfield, Ill.: Charles C Thomas, 1981.

Polansky, Norman, Rebecca J. Cabral, Stephen Magura, and Michael H. Phillips. "Comparative Norms for the Childhood Level of Living Scale." *Journal of Social Service Research* 6, no. 3/4 (spring/summer 1983):45–55.

Van Meter, Mary Jane S. Letters to the author, March 27, 1985; July 22, 1985; September 5, 1985.

Van Meter, Mary Jane S. Telephone conversation with the author, July 9, 1985.

Appendix
Summary of Home-Based, Family-Centered Programs

Program (Year Begun)	Geographic Area	Referral Source	Population Served	Hrs. Direct Service/Wk.	24-hr. Avail.
Center for Family Life, St. Christopher's Home Brooklyn, New York (1978)	Urban	Social service agencies Schools Court Relatives of clients Self-referrals	Families with a child under 18 and pregnant women residing in the Sunset Park area of Brooklyn mostly low-income, single-parent or reconstituted families	Varies greatly from 1–20 hrs./wk., depending on family need and treatment modalities used	Yes
Intensive Family Services (IFS), Children's Services Division, Ore. (1980)	Urban Rural Suburban	Children's Services Division	Family in which a child is approved for out-of-home placement	Approx. 2 hrs./ wk., mostly in-home	No
High Impact Services, Children's Services Division, Ore. (1982)	Urban Rural Suburban	Children's Services Division	Family first entering the state child welfare system	Approx. 2 hrs./ wk., mostly in-home	No

Primary Treatment Modalities	Indiv. or Team Approach	No. of Cases per Counselor	Av. Length of Treatment	No. of Families per Year	FY 85–86 Budget	Cost per Family per Year
Individual, group, and family counseling Family life education Advocacy clinic and emergency food program Foster grandparent program Big brother/big sister program Recreational activities School-based program Job counseling and placement School-age child care, school-based activity program	Both	Varies	30 days– 3 years	662	$1,000,000	Not calculated
Family therapy, may utilize the following schools of thought: multiple-impact therapy structural family therapy strategic family therapy communications theory Collaboration with appropriate community resources	Team (each family has a primary therapist and a secondary therapist)	8.37 families per therapist	3 months	1,188	Budget is part of the Children's Services Division budget	$1,131.85
Family therapy, may utilize the following schools of thought: multiple-impact therapy	Team (each family has a primary therapist and a secondary therapist)	11 families per therapist	3 months	1,804	Budget is part of the Children's Services Division budget	Not calculated

Program (Year Begun)	Geographic Area	Referral Source	Population Served	Hrs. Direct Service/Wk.	24-hr. Avail.
High Impact Services (continued)					
Head Start, Brockton, Mass. (1965)	Urban Rural Suburban	Public schools Private agencies Pediatricians Pediatric hospitals Self-referrals	Families with 3–4 year-old children 90% from single-parent homes 90% meet poverty guidelines	Center-based: 16 hrs./wk., Home-based: 3.25 hrs./wk. Summer program: 20 hrs./ wk.	No
Home and Community Treatment, Mendota Mental Health Institute, Madison, Wisc. (1969)	Urban Suburban Small percentage of rural areas	Private practitioners Clinics Schools Social service agencies	Families with 3–10-year-old children with emotional and behavioral problems 90% Caucasian 40% intact families 60% single parent Primarily working class	In-home: 4 hrs./wk. Office: 2 hrs./ wk.	No
Homebuilders, Behavioral Sciences Institute, Federal Way, Wash. (1974)	Urban Rural Suburban	Washington State Department of Social and Health Services	Primarily Caucasian 47% single parent 32% step-parent and blended 21% two natural parents	10.8 hrs./wk. direct service 6.1 hrs./wk. collateral service	Yes

Primary Treatment Modalities	Indiv. or Team Approach	No. of Cases per Counselor	Av. Length of Treatment	No. of Families per Year	FY 85–86 Budget	Cost per Family per Year
structural family therapy strategic family therapy communications theory Collaboration with appropriate community resources						
Empowerment Educational services Family support and advocacy: health services parent involvement advocacy and networking with community resources	Indiv.	not available	1–2 years	530	$1,724,178	Center-based: $2,598 Home-based: $2,106
Systems approach Social learning theory Behavior management	Team (4 staff members)	1 team serves 6 families	15 months	12	$150,000	$11,250
Client-centered therapy Behavior and emotion management Behavioral rehearsal Communication skill-building Rational emotive therapy Crisis intervention Territorial approach to human relations Concrete services	Primarily indiv.; team as necessary	2 families per therapist	4–6 wks.	359 (481 children targeted for placement)	$1,069,000	$1,980 (average cost per child)

Program (Year Begun)	Geographic Area	Referral Source	Population Served	Hrs. Direct Service/Wk.	24-hr. avail.
Family Based Service, Crittenton Family Support Center, Youth Service, Inc., Philadelphia, Penn. (1974)	Urban	Philadelphia County Children and Youth Agency	Most families referred because of emotional or physical abuse and neglect ½ of the families are court-involved All families are on public assistance, SSI, or social security ⅓ have an adult male in the home 74% black 20% Caucasian 4% Hispanic 2% interracial	2–10 hrs./wk. (average of 4 hrs./wk.)	Yes
In-Home Family Counseling/Support Services, Iowa Children's & Family Services, Des Moines, Iowa (1977)	Urban Rural Suburban	Department of Human Services Juvenile Court Employee assistance programs Self-referrals	Primarily Caucasian Mostly low income Many socially isolated, rural families 50% single parent	6 hrs./wk. (3 hrs. in-home)	Yes
Lower East Side Family Union (LESFU), New York, New York (1972)	Urban	Various	Families with at least one child under 18 and pregnant women 90% on public assistance 45% Hispanic 35% Chinese 20% black and Caucasian	20 hrs./wk.	No; soon to be implemented

Primary Treatment Modalities	Indiv. or Team Approach	No. of Cases per Counselor	Av. Length of Treatment	No. of Families per Year	FY 85–86 Budget	Cost per Family per Year
Concrete and psychological services Systems and developmental approach, within ecological framework Interventions include individual, couple, family, extended family, and crisis counseling Concrete interventions Linkages with community resources Life skills education Parent support groups	Both	10–12 families per social worker; 6 families per family care worker	20 months	125	$423,524	$6,000–$6,500
Individual, marital, and structural family counseling Teaching Role modeling Family advocacy Networking with community resources (ecological model)	Indiv.	4–7 families per counselor; 1–4 families per supervisory staff	6 months	297	$883,000	$2,737
Case management Coordinate, integrate, and monitor community services Direct services (e.g., homemaking, counseling, and advocacy)	Team	Social work associate: 15 families Family worker: 8 families	18 months	350	$1,000,000	$2,250

Program (Year Begun)	Geographic Area	Referral Source	Population Served	Hrs. Direct Service/Wk.	24-hr. avail.
Maine Home-Based Services, Maine (1980)	Urban Rural Suburban	Various	Families with a child 0–20 years of age; children 9–15 a priority	3–6 hrs./wk. direct service; 6–11 hrs./wk. collateral service	Yes
Parents and Children Together (PACT), Detroit, Mich. (1977)	Urban	Children and Youth Services of the Michigan/Wayne County Department of Social Services	All substantiated cases of child abuse or neglect Most single-parent and on public assistance 75% black	2 hrs./wk. direct service, plus additional support services	Yes

Primary Treatment Modalities	Indiv. or Team Approach	No. of Cases per Counselor	Av. Length of Treatment	No. of Families per Year	FY 85–86 Budget	Cost per Family per Year
Educate Act as role models Link with formal and informal resources Each program employs its own treatment modalities	Team	1 team serves 3–6 families	9–12 wks.	24–48	$130,000– $150,000	$3,125– $6,250
Provision of concrete services Realistic goal setting Behavior management Accessing and coordinating community resources Education	Indiv.	8 families per student	8.1 months	318	$610,000	$1,900

12
A Comprehensive Program Model

Based on a comprehensive review of the literature, past programs, and programs currently operating, this chapter recommends a generic program model. The difficulty inherent in suggesting such a model must be recognized. Preceding chapters have presented a number of programs that cover different populations and geographic areas and that offer different treatment modalities and employ paraprofessionals, professionals, or a combination of both types of staff. The reader should closely examine the programs and adapt the most useful aspects of each for the intended target population and geographic area.

The General Goals of a Family-Centered Program

A counselor first overcomes the cycle of suspicion, rejection, failure, and withdrawal that hinders multiproblem families. Believing in a family, being accepting, and giving them hope that they can change is fundamental to effective treatment. Directness and honesty are also crucial in establishing a trusting, respectful relationship. A counselor who is constantly accessible (on call twenty-four hours a day, seven days a week), who frequently calls and makes home visits, and who schedules appointments at times convenient for the family shows family members they are worthwhile and that there is hope. As a trusting relationship is built, the gap between the family and the community lessens.

Home-based counseling helps overcome the family's resistance to counseling. A multiproblem family is less intimidated by a counselor who comes to their home. A counselor observes the family in its own environment, and thereby obtains valuable first-hand information that would have been inaccessible in office visits. When a family has no transportation, in-home counseling makes counseling possible.

Establishing a positive relationship is key to treatment. The counselor's goal is to become a trusted, accepting friend rather than a professional who is there to judge the home environment and solve family problems. A counselor does not begin by offering a treatment contract. At least initially, most families are threatened by any formal treatment. Trust develops as the counselor serves as friend, teacher, nurturer, role model, advocate, and facilitator.

Empowerment is a major goal that threads its way through all treatment modalities. The counselor and the family work as partners to solve problems, enhance family strengths, and resolve family difficulties. Instead of acting according to a preconceived notion of the family's problems, the counselor listens to what the family says its problems are and encourages family members to prioritize their needs. Parents often feel powerless and hopeless; thus, it is critical to put them in charge by involving them from the very beginning in planning treatment. Head Start is the best example of a program designed to empower families; parent participation is encouraged in all aspects of the program. Parents make decisions about program operation; they take part in the classroom as paid employees, volunteers, or observers; they plan and participate in activities specifically for Head Start parents; and they also work closely with Head Start staff to learn how to help their own children. Many parents have dramatically improved their lives as a result of their involvement with Head Start.

The potential of multiproblem families is often underutilized and undervalued as a result of societal stigma and problem-focused interventions. Building on family strengths by emphasizing their positive qualities is an important aspect of treatment. Recognizing and enhancing the strengths of a particular ethnic group is especially useful. Billingsley and Hill describe this approach as it relates to black families, and in their book on ethnicity and family therapy, McGoldrick, Pearce, and Giordano discuss a number of ethnic groups.[1]

The counselor searches for the strengths of each family member. These strengths may be difficult to find, but they are present. By drawing out and building on a family's assets, the counselor promotes self-confidence and offers hope that the family's situation can improve.

Service provision is not based solely on rehabilitation or remediation; it also has a developmental focus. From this viewpoint, a multiproblem family is perceived as deficient in certain skills that can be promoted through education and skill or resource development.[2] It is more constructive for a counselor to regard a family as lacking in alternatives or education than to assume the presence of pathology. The family may have ineffective problem-solving techniques or poor coping skills, or it may not know how to use community resources to meet its needs. A counselor nurtures the family and teaches family members new, positive ways to address recurrent problems. The counselor concentrates on increasing the family's ability to solve problems, building family strengths, and facilitating the family's ability to advocate on its own behalf.

The environment in which many multiproblem families live must not be overlooked. Severe environmental problems such as low income, crime, drug abuse, lack of housing or poor housing, and health problems have great impact on families' daily lives. When a family resides in a very stressful environment, its problems are greatly exacerbated. Environmental and personal problems cannot be separated.

Assessing and addressing the concrete difficulties of a family is the family counselor's first priority.[3] If a mother is beset by a number of problems and is unable to meet her own needs or those of her children, she feels overwhelmed and hopeless. The counselor helps the mother deal with the problems she faces every day. This may entail helping her find a job or a place to live.

Often family members expect to fail, even at concrete tasks; the tasks initially assigned must be small. For example, if a mother rarely leaves the house, one of the first goals of treatment is to convince her to go to a local restaurant with the counselor for coffee. After doing this a few times, the counselor takes the mother grocery shopping. Setting small goals makes a task more manageable and creates an environment in which success is likely. Because the counselor's expectation is achievable, the client is not once again faced with failure. When a family member succeeds at a task, the counselor recognizes and reinforces the achievement in order to encourage additional successes, raise the client's self-esteem, and improve his or her ability to negotiate the environment. Repeated success enables people to develop hope and confidence in themselves.

When used as the sole treatment, traditional talk therapy is ineffectual with multiproblem families. A counselor must be available to help the family paint their kitchen or teach the mother how to drive a car, find housing, and obtain day care; these activities are the foundation of a trusting relationship. Successfully coping with day-to-day needs gives the family a sense of accomplishment as well as the motivation to address more complex problems.

By providing concrete assistance and responding to immediate concerns first, the counselor demonstrates genuine concern and shows the family that he or she can help. In this way, the worker gains the family's acceptance. While establishing a strong relationship, the counselor lays the groundwork for more complex interactions; intrapsychic and interpersonal issues can then become the focus of attention. Complex issues can be discussed only after the resistance of family members has broken down and the counselor has established a deeper relationship with the family.

The more skillfully family members can resolve concrete and emotional problems, the better they can address interpersonal issues. As family members learn and use more effective interpersonal skills among themselves, their skills generalize to relationships outside of the family.

Without concrete assistance, even the best psychiatric counseling will fail. Research studies have concluded that effective counseling addresses concrete as well as psychological needs.[4] "In many of these families, material poverty and poverty in interpersonal experience are part of a heritage that has been handed down from generation to generation. Help is often needed on both fronts, but with an understanding of how the one affects the other."[5]

Specific Treatment Approaches

Using a systems approach within an ecological framework is recommended for those working with multiproblem families.[6] An ecological systems approach can be used in combination with a structural approach, strategic approach, communication theory, social learning theory, or reality therapy. Programs that employ different treatment modalities are equally effective. The most important component of effective treatment is not a specific approach or technique; it is the establishment of a trusting relationship between the counselor and the family. No matter which approach is taken, the counselor must convey authenticity, sensitivity, acceptance, and flexibility, with the primary goal of teaching families how to cope.

A structural family therapy approach is well suited for work with multiproblem families.[7] Training staff in this approach provides them with a clear, concrete, and highly useful framework from which to assess and treat these families. Structural family therapy is advantageous because it takes the focus off the identified client and puts the parents in charge. It identifies the hierarchical organization in a family and focuses on the family's style of communication.

The strategic approach, through emphasizing family structure, addresses the presenting problem by altering the way the family is organized. Like structural family therapy, the strategic approach emphasizes family hierarchy and putting parents in charge of their children. The counselor should try more direct approaches before using strategic therapy; however, if these methods prove ineffectual, the strategic approach can circumvent issues that block a family's ability to change. This approach escalates a family's pain, as opposed to decreasing it.[8] Strategic therapy is not useful for all multiproblem families; it must be used by counselors who thoroughly understand the approach and use it discriminately.

Communication theory is an integral aspect of family treatment because dysfunctional communication blocks effective problem-solving. Families with communication problems have difficulty communicating internally as well as externally. The importance of clear, direct communication has been addressed by a number of authors. Satir's discussion of communication theory is useful in working with multiproblem families, as are Minuchin's structural interventions to regulate family communication.[9] Alexander and Parsons present techniques that improve family communication and demonstrate how improved communication enhances family functioning.[10]

Social learning theory involving a behavioral systems model may also be employed. The behavioral management approach comes from learning theory and focuses on the presenting problems. This approach has proved effective in a number of programs.[11] A behavioral model has several advantages. It establishes clear, measurable, and concrete goals, so that progress is visible and an environment in which success is likely is created. The model assumes that parents need to assess their parenting skills and obtain new skills to improve their parenting ability. Pathology is not the focus; parents who are weak in certain skills can learn specific techniques to enhance parent-child interaction. In addition, the model enables the family to control the reward/punishment process. Once a behavioral design has been established, family members can follow it on their own, and can gauge progress by themselves. Parents resume the authority over their children that, in many cases, they had considered lost.

One of the advantages of working with parents in their homes is that they are shown how to employ a behavioral plan in the setting in which the plan will be used; they do not have to translate discussions from the office to the home environment. The counselor serves as a role model, teaching parents how to follow the behavioral plan, watching them practice, and providing reinforcement.

Home and Community Treatment, a program of Mendota Mental Health Institute in Wisconsin, takes a predominately behavioral approach. Child management programs are individually developed for each family. Demonstration, modeling, and coaching are emphasized for parents, teachers, and children.

Role modeling is not used only in social learning theory, but is also an important aspect of most programs serving multiproblem families. A counselor constantly teaches parents and children by demonstrating new behavior patterns and ways of coping. By negotiating differences during a family meeting, talking with a youngster during a recreational activity, or accompanying a mother to the Housing Authority, the counselor serves as a model for the family.

Reality therapy is employed by a number of programs. A counselor recognizes that family members are unable to meet their basic needs and, within the context of a caring relationship, helps them fulfill those needs. In his book, *Reality Therapy,* Glasser points out that the counselor must become involved with the client, otherwise there is no therapy. Once a relationship is established, the counselor helps family members face reality. They recognize that their behavior has prevented them from meeting their needs. This approach is very much analogous to reparenting, in that the counselor establishes a genuine relationship with the client, continually validates the client, and helps him or her become a "responsible" person. Reality therapy focuses on the present as opposed to the past, and emphasizes behavioral, not attitudinal change.

Studies repeatedly indicate that comprehensive, multidimensional interventions are more effective than a single method.[12] Multiproblem families need a number of intensive support services. A neighborhood program, such as the Center for Family Life in Sunset Park, which provides a vast array of developmental and rehabilitative services, is ideal. This program affects families in more ways than any other program reviewed, but because of the high costs, most programs are unable to offer such extensive and diverse services. In addition, most programs are not neighborhood-oriented; they lack a strong investment and involvement in the communities they serve. Working with families without recognizing and addressing larger social problems is unrealistic.

Maintaining an Ecological Approach: Establishing a Coordinated Service Delivery System

A cooperative human service delivery system is established to avoid fragmented, crisis-oriented service provision. Service delivery linkages reflect a coordinated approach involving all agencies and significant individuals with which a family has contact. Usually, families have been referred from one agency to another, with each agency assuming temporary responsibility but none providing continuing, coherent services. Responsibility for service delivery must be centralized in one agency to insure coordination of treatment, comprehensive service delivery, and service continuity.

When a worker (or team) assumes responsibility for a family, he or she clarifies the roles of each involved agency. The Lower East Side Family Union, for example, establishes and monitors contracts with all the agencies with which families interact. Most programs recognize that it is ludicrous for an agency serving multiproblem families to work in isolation.

The necessity of having the community behind a project for multiproblem families cannot be overstated. Family work is only effective if backed by community support; operating in isolation is needlessly limiting. Before a project is initiated, community agencies must be invested in the program, and their support must be maintained throughout the project. Such support not only ensures the project's survival, but also promotes coordinated services. A number of programs recognize the importance of community support and have developed ways to maintain community involvement. For example, the St. Paul Family-Centered Project, a twenty-year research and demonstration project (1948–1968), was based on the principle of community organization. It recognized that community support was intrinsic to program success, and seven agencies joined together to loan workers to the project. In addition, the project was responsible to a committee of lay and professional people. Community organization and direct service were key program components.

Like the St. Paul Family-Centered Project, Maine's home-based programs emphasize the principle of community organization. Each of the nine home-based services funded by the Department of Mental Health and Mental Retardation has a multiagency, regional advisory committee composed of representatives from all child and family agencies or resources within the program's geographic area. The committee holds monthly meetings that provide a forum for networking, help members understand referral criteria and procedures, prevent inappropriate referrals, and enable members to more clearly understand each other's roles and responsibilities. If there are problems in making a referral to a community resource, local service providers are invested in the program by virtue of their membership on the advisory committee, and are accessible for problem resolution. Advisory committees encourage cooperation among agencies, and they have been intrinsic to the success of Maine's family preservation programs.

Taking an ecological approach is critical because environmental forces strongly affect families. Community resources and psychological treatment are offered together. Typically, the influence of the environment on a family is ignored or, at best, overlooked.[13] Attention should be focused on environmental problems first. As part of assessment and treatment, significant individuals or agencies involved with the family are contacted. They provide the counselor with a holistic understanding of the family. The counselor works with these significant others to ensure coordinated service provision. Working with a family in isolation encourages the family to become dependent on the counselor. Throughout treatment, the counselor acts as role model and advocate, and teaches family members to access informal and formal community resources to meet their needs.[14]

Initially, a counselor may need to accompany family members when they access services. By showing a family how to use a particular service, the family worker takes the family through the steps of a process that, once learned, can be used to resolve future problems. "What an individual learns about his ability to effect change in his own life may be of far greater significance than the change itself."[15] The counselor involves and orchestrates a wide array of resources by penetrating bureaucracies and establishing successful linkages for families.

The importance of informal help must not be overlooked, and a number of authors have emphasized this point. "Some families manage to hold themselves together by a network of intimate interrelationships of mutual aid and social integration with their neighbors and kin."[16] Studies indicate that "formal services provided by professionals . . . often failed to make effective use of informal helping resources. . . . both formal and informal help can be blended together to capitalize on the advantages and potency of each. Exclusive reliance on either . . . is less reasonable than an appropriate balance of both."[17]

Support Groups: Adjuncts to Family Counseling

Parent support groups are educational, therapeutic, and recreational; they are invaluable adjuncts to family counseling. The groups decrease the social and sometimes geographic isolation of many parents and encourage interpersonal interaction. Through such groups, parents receive support from their peers, learn how to assume responsibility and set behavioral limits for their children, and get advice on how to deal with their own problems. In this way, parents develop a mutual support system and often make friends whom they see socially, creating an informal social network.[18]

Through participation in a group, the parent's world is broadened emotionally, socially, and even geographically. The group introduces new experiences to parents who rarely leave their community, and often takes them on excursions out of the immediate neighborhood. The group also offers a parent the opportunity to help other parents resolve their problems, a role that is often unfamiliar.

Adolescent support groups, composed of youngsters from multiproblem families, complement family counseling. In such groups, youths discuss pressing issues, confront their peers, find support, and develop friendships. Group meetings are held at offices and at recreational sites. Participating in group activities that necessitate teamwork (for example, modified outward bound events, mountain climbing, or building a house) teaches youngsters to work together, negotiate differences, and rely on each other. It also offers tangible accomplishments of which they can be proud.

Taking pictures of and/or videotaping youths in outdoor programs provides visible reinforcement of their accomplishments and enables adolescents and their families to view events together. Placing adolescents in helping roles is also valuable; a community service program is established in which youth work, in some capacity, with individuals who require assistance (such as younger children, the elderly, the retarded, or the handicapped). Characterized as bad, impossible, and crazy, these youngsters are unused to giving help, whereas they are intimately acquainted with being the recipient of services. Through such programs, youths' self-worth is enhanced and negative labels are challenged.

Creating a Sense of Community within the Program

Creating a strong community feeling—an esprit de corps—within a family counseling program is vital. A community network may be developed by having a program newsletter, holding family get-togethers, offering family field trips, or showing slides of trips taken by youngsters and/or parents. Representatives from community resources are invited to attend gatherings in order to promote communication among staff, families, and the community. Through such gatherings, the families interact with community representatives in an informal, unthreatening setting. Community representatives are able to see multiproblem families in a positive light, which allows them to reconsider the negative labels these families have carried for so many years.

Many programs fail to develop a strong sense of community, because they have never considered doing so, or because they do not think it is important, or because they feel it is unprofessional. A family counseling program serves as a family's extended family, and is thus a significant formal and informal resource. Creating community feeling facilitates positive feelings among families and between families and the community; it also encourages socializing among families and counteracts their fear and mistrust of the community.

Short-Term versus Long-Term Program Models

A major question in designing a program to serve multiproblem families is: should the program be short- or long-term? Which is most effective? These questions are difficult to answer. The short-term programs (under six months) reviewed in this book include High Impact Services and the Intensive Family Services Program, Homebuilders, and Maine Home-Based Services. The long-term programs (six months or longer) include the Center for Family Life, Family Based Service of Youth Service, Inc.; Head Start; Home and Community Treatment of Mendota Mental Health Institute; In-Home Family Counseling/Support Services of Iowa Children's and Family Services; the Lower East Side Family Union; and Parents and Children Together. Long- and short-term programs have different goals; both have proved effective. Both types of program focus on the relationship between the counselor and the family and provide intensive services. Whether to employ a short- or long-term model depends on what the program is intended to accomplish.

The short-term model provides *intervention*. In this model, the crisis is important. A crisis indicates that the family is at the boiling point; something above the general level of family dysfunction has erupted and the family is threatened with having a child removed. Short-term programs defuse the crisis at hand and provide the family with the skills to resolve future crises on its own. A short-term program will also link the family with community resources that will help it meet its long-term needs.

A short-term program is advantageous in that the time limit provides the family and the counselor with an incentive to work together intensively for a brief, predetermined period of time. Both parties know from the beginning exactly how long treatment will last. When in a crisis, a family is highly motivated to change; family members are more willing to experiment with new behaviors because they are in so much pain. The threat of the removal of a child also motivates the family to accept services. By helping a family in a crisis, the counselor creates a bond with the family, which increases the likelihood of successfully teaching the family to cope effectively. Another benefit of the short-term model is that it discourages a dependent relationship between counselor and family.

The short-term model presents three major areas of concern, which must be acknowledged by those considering model adaptation. One concern is the very tight time frame. Is it possible to develop a significant relationship with a multiproblem family within such a short time? Families that have been involved with numerous agencies have developed a negative attitude toward social workers. How can resistance be overcome so quickly? A family's negative patterns have developed over a period of years, sometimes generations; how much long-range impact can short-term treatment have? A second concern is that although short-term programs may effectively resolve crises, as a result of their brevity, the interventions fail to address or only touch the surface of deeper, more pervasive problems. A third concern is how well families respond when referred to resources within the community, either during treatment or at termination. How effective is it to have established a trusting relationship with a multiproblem family for an intensive period of time, only to refer the family, after a few weeks, to traditional services? Most agencies do not give special attention to multiproblem families. Can most families make the transition and benefit from community services, or do they regress and revert back to familiar patterns? The Maine Department of Mental Health and Mental Retardation recognized this potential problem and mandated each of its nine home-based programs to establish an advisory committee composed of representatives from all child and family agencies or resources in the program's geographic area. This committee serves many purposes, one of which is to act as a resource if there are problems in effecting a referral. All local service providers have representatives on the committee who are available to resolve problems. Maine's ability to foresee and obviate the problems in linking families with local agencies is impressive.

In the long-term model, intervention is not limited to the presenting crisis; staff become intensively involved in the deep-seated problems that have characterized a family over a period of years—sometimes generations. Because of the previously cited concerns about short-term intervention, the use of long-term *treatment,* as opposed to intervention, is strongly recommended. If gains are going to be made, they will take time. Long-term programs give the counselor and the family enough time to develop a trusting relationship. It takes a while for multiproblem families to establish real relationships with their counselors. Eight to twelve weeks, although intensive, is not enough time to develop a trusting relationship. Such a relationship is difficult to establish and, once established, it must exist for a significant period of time to be considered solid.

The long-term programs also have inherent drawbacks. The usefulness of treatment must be continually assessed to guard against prolonging treatment over too long a period. Another drawback is that the intense relationship between counselor and family makes termination difficult. Termination must be carefully planned, and the possibility of a dependent relationship between counselor and family needs to be addressed. Family members must be affiliated with community resources to ensure treatment continuity and decrease dependency.

The Individual Approach versus the Team Approach

Another major question to ask when developing a program is whether an individual or a team approach should be employed. Some programs use one approach or the other, and some employ either, based on the family served. Programs primarily using an individual approach include Head Start, Homebuilders, In-Home Family Counseling/Support Services of Iowa Children's and Family Services, and Parents and Children Together. Programs primarily using a team approach include High Impact Services and Intensive Family Services Program, Home and Community Treatment of Mendota Mental Health Institute, the Lower East Side Family Union, and Maine Home-Based Services. The Center for Family Life and Family Based Service of Youth Service, Inc., employ either an individual or a team approach, depending on the family. There are a number of different types of team approaches. Family Based Service of Youth Service, Inc. uses a team approach in which each team member—a social worker and a family care worker—provides different services. The social worker's responsibilities include counseling, case management, linking families with community resources, and supervising the family care worker. The family care worker works closely with the family, and helps in the day-to-day management of the children and the household. Maine Home-Based Services has team members who work together to provide concrete and psychological services. Home and Community Treatment at Mendota Mental Health Institute uses interdisciplinary teams; each team is composed of an occupational therapist, a nurse, and psychologist. The diverse viewpoints of the team members enhance assessment and treatment.

One advantage of the individual approach is that one person establishes a trusting relationship with a family. Considering a multiproblem family's distrust of social workers, it is more likely that a family will establish one, rather than two or more, relationships. An individual approach is also more economical.

The advantages of a team approach are numerous. Having a team work with the family minimizes the possibility that the counselors will become overwhelmed, and minimizes stress and burnout. The team members not only provide extra support for a family, they also support and encourage each other. Team members act as role models by showing a family how people work together to solve problems. Having a male-female team is especially useful; it demonstrates how the two sexes can share and negotiate problems. Programs working with a minority population may assign a team that includes one member of the same race or ethnicity as the family. This practice helps establish a trusting relationship. A team is also useful when a family subsystem or a family member can benefit from individual treatment.

Working with a multiproblem family is difficult because so many things happen in the family. Working in a team enables counselors to maintain their objectivity and provide each other with different viewpoints on how to assess and treat family problems and how to build on family strengths. If one team member has problems working with a family member, another team member can assist. If a team member is ill, on vacation, or leaves the job, the family has an established relationship with the other member(s) of the team, which insures treatment continuity. The team approach diminishes the extent to which a family can become dependent on one service provider by enabling the family to establish more than one intensive, trusting relationship.

A team approach also has disadvantages. A family may pit team members against each other. A team's efficacy depends on the counselors working cooperatively toward the same goals. In addition, a team approach is more costly than an individual approach.

Both a team and an individual approach are valuable, but it is suggested that a team approach be the primary method of service delivery. However, a program using a team approach should be flexible, so that treatment can be tailored to each family's needs. For example, Family Based Service of Youth Service, Inc., has clear, specific criteria for case assignment that determine whether an individual or team approach is employed.

After termination formal follow-up services are usually not provided to families. It is important, however, to let families know that they can contact the program to obtain assistance or to let the program know how they're progressing.

Notes

The full citations for the author and date references can be found in the Annotated Bibliography.

Introduction

1. See Bryce 1981; Carter and McGoldrick 1980; Cautley 1979; Clark, Zalis, and Sacco 1982; Hoffman and Long 1969; Janzen and Harris 1980; Meyerstein 1977; Overton and Tinker 1978; Reissman 1973; Selig 1976; Thorman 1982.

2. See Auerswald 1968, p. 214.

3. See Auerswald 1968; Jacobi 1968.

4. See Bryce 1981; Minuchin 1970a; Wolock et al. 1979.

5. See Bryce 1981; Lloyd and Bryce 1984; Minuchin 1970a; Wolock et al. 1979.

6. See Bronfenbrenner 1981, p. 40.

7. See Alexander 1974; Bryce 1981; Burt 1976a, 1976b; Cautley and Plane 1983; Compher 1983; Hutchinson 1983; Jones 1976, 1983; Kahn and Kamerman 1975; Knitzer and Allen 1978; Lloyd and Bryce 1984; Maybanks and Bryce 1979; Sudia 1982; Wolock et al. 1979. Also, Jill McCleave Kinney, Barbara Madsen, Thomas Fleming, and David Haapala, "Homebuilders: Keeping Families Together," *Journal of Consulting and Clinical Psychology* 45, no. 4 (Aug. 1977).

8. See Alexander 1974; Klein, Alexander, and Parsons 1977. Also, David Haapala, "Perceived Helpfulness, Attributed Critical Incident Responsibility, and a Discrimination of Home Based Family Therapy Treatment Outcomes: Homebuilders Model." (Tacoma, Wash.: Catholic Community Services; Federal Way, Wash.: Behavioral Sciences Institute, Nov. 1983.) Photocopy.

9. See Birt 1956; Brown 1968; Buell and Associates 1952; Geismar and La Sorte 1964.

10. See Buell and Associates 1952.

11. See Birt 1956, p. 42.

12. See Jacobi 1968, p. 67.

Chapter 1

1. See Aponte 1976b, p. 433.
2. See Geismar and La Sorte 1964.
3. See Knitzer and Allen 1978, p. 49.
4. See Schlesinger 1963, p. 38.
5. See Auerswald 1972; Compton 1979b; Hoffman and Long 1969; Jacobi 1968; Janzen and Harris 1980; King and Rabinowitz 1965; Mannino and Shore 1972; Meyerstein 1977; Minuchin 1970a; Overton and Tinker 1978; Selig 1976.
6. Edward Hinckley, "Homebuilders: Home Treatment for Families." Paper presented at the Community Program Innovations conference, Community-Based Programming; Approaches for Increasing Autonomy, Empowerment and Independence, Boston, June 1984.
7. See Compton 1979b, p. 7.

Chapter 2

1. Jill Kinney and David Haapala, "Prevention of Violence in In-Home Family Crisis Intervention." No date. Photocopy.
2. See Schlesinger 1963.
3. See Barnhill 1979; Carter and McGoldrick 1980; Lewis et al. 1976; Walsh 1982.
4. See Barnhill 1979, p. 96.
5. See Satir 1972, p. 22.
6. Kierkegaard, Søren, *Fear and Trembling and the Sickness unto Death.* (Princeton, N.J.: Princeton University Press, 1941), p. 165.

Chapter 3

1. See Butehorn 1978.
2. See Ford and Herrick 1974.
3. See Minuchin 1974.

Chapter 5

1. See Overton and Tinker 1978, p. 65.
2. Jill Kinney, David Haapala, and Joan Elizabeth Gast, "Assessment of Families in Crisis, in *Treating Families in the Home: An Alternative to Placement,* edited by Marvin Bryce and June C. Lloyd. (Springfield, Ill.: Charles C Thomas, 1981).
3. See Kamerman and Kahn 1976, p. 217.

4. See Aponte 1976a, p. 311.

5. See Alexander 1974; Aponte 1976a, 1976b, 1977; Auerswald 1968, 1972; Carter and McGoldrick 1980; Compton 1979b; Gatti and Colman 1976; Geismar 1971a; Geismar and Krisberg 1967; Hartman and Laird 1983; Hoffman and Long 1969; Janzen and Harris 1980; Lloyd and Bryce 1984; Mannino and Shore 1972; Meyerstein 1977; Minuchin 1970a, 1970b; Orcott 1977; Powell 1980; Taylor and Carithers 1976; Umbarger 1972; Woodbury and Woodbury 1969.

Chapter 6

1. See Bryce 1981; Clark, Zalis, and Sacco 1982; Compton 1979b; Edna McConnell Clark Foundation 1985; Epstein and Shainline 1974; Janzen and Harris 1980; Lawder, Poulin, and Andrews 1984; McKinney 1970; Minuchin 1970a; Overton and Tinker 1978; Reichler, Babigian, and Gardner 1966; Reissman 1973; Schlachter 1975; Taylor and Carithers 1976; Wolock et al. 1979; Woodbury and Woodbury 1969.

2. See Maybanks and Bryce 1979, p. 276.

Chapter 7

1. See Bryce 1981; Carter and McGoldrick 1980; Compton 1979b; Geismar 1971b; Geismar and Krisberg 1967; Halper and Jones 1981; Hutchinson 1983; Janzen and Harris 1980; Jones, Magura, and Shyne 1981; Jones, Newman, and Shyne 1976; Lawder, Poulin, and Andrews 1984; Lloyd and Bryce 1984; Rabin, Sens, and Rosenbaum 1982.

2. See Lloyd and Bryce 1984.

3. See Jones, Magura, and Shyne 1981.

4. See Lloyd and Bryce 1984, p. 61.

5. See Aponte 1977; Bryce 1981; Cautely 1979; Compher 1983; Compton 1962, 1979b; Geismar 1971a; Goldstein 1973; Halper and Jones 1981; Hartman and Laird 1983; Hill 1971; Kinch 1979; Lloyd and Bryce 1984; Minuchin 1970a; Overton and Tinker 1978; Schlesinger 1963; Sudia 1982; Taylor 1972.

6. See Bryce 1981; Clark, Zalis, and Sacco 1982; Overton and Tinker 1978.

7. See Minuchin et al. 1967, p. 293.

8. See Pittman 1977, p. 15.

9. See Epstein and Shainline 1974; Goldstein 1973; Halper and Jones 1981; Janzen and Harris 1980; McKinney 1970; Morse et al. 1977; Taylor 1972; Taylor and Carithers 1976; Thorman 1982.

Chapter 9

1. See U.S. Department of Health and Human Services 1981, p. 1.

2. See Epstein and Shainline 1974, p. 234.

3. Edward Hinckley, "Homebuilders: Home Treatment for Families." Paper presented at the Community Program Innovations conference, Community-Based Programming: Approaches for Increasing Autonomy, Empowerment and Independence, Boston, June 1984.

4. See Chestang 1978, p. 37.

Chapter 10

1. See DeWitt 1978; Halpern 1984; Janzen and Harris 1980; Masten 1979; Parsons and Alexander 1973. Also, David Haapala, "Perceived Helpfulness, Attributed Critical Incident Responsibility, and a Discrimination of Home Based Family Therapy Treatment Outcomes: Homebuilders Model." (Tacoma, Wash.: Catholic Community Services; Federal Way, Wash.: Behavioral Sciences Institute, Nov. 1984.) Photocopy.

2. See DeWitt 1978; Gilbert, Christensen, and Margolin 1984.

3. See Parsons and Alexander 1973.

4. See Klein, Alexander, and Parsons 1977.

5. See Maybanks and Bryce 1979, p. 332.

Chapter 12

1. See Billingsley 1969; Hill 1971; McGoldrick, Pearce, and Giordano 1982.

2. See Clark, Zalis, and Sacco 1982; Compher 1983; McKinney 1970.

3. See Chilman 1966; Clark, Zalis, and Sacco 1982; Geismar and Krisberg 1967; Halper and Jones 1981; McKinney 1970; Rabin, Sens, and Rosenbaum 1982.

4. See Geismar 1971b; Jones 1976; Jones, Magura, and Shyne 1981; Jones, Newman, and Shyne 1976.

5. See Cade 1975, p. 142.

6. See Auerswald 1968, 1972; Carter and McGoldrick 1980; Halper and Jones 1981; Heying 1985; Hoffman and Long 1969; Lloyd and Bryce 1984; Maybanks and Bryce 1979; Mannino and Shore 1972; Umbarger 1972.

7. See Carter and McGoldrick 1980; Minuchin 1974; Minuchin et al. 1967.

8. Eric Emery, telephone conversation with the author, September 10, 1985.

9. See Satir 1967; Minuchin 1974; Minuchin and Montalvo 1967; Minuchin et al. 1967.

10. See Alexander 1973, 1974; Alexander and Parsons 1973; Parsons and Alexander 1973.

11. See Alexander 1973, 1974; Alexander and Parsons 1973; Cautley 1979; Parsons and Alexander 1973. Also, Mary Ann Fahl, "Shaping Parent-Child Interactions: A Behavioral Model in a Family Context," in *Treating Families in the Home: An Alternative to Placement,* edited by Marvin Bryce and June C. Lloyd. (Springfield, Ill.: Charles C Thomas, 1981.

12. See Geismar 1971b; Janzen and Harris 1980; Jones, Magura, and Shyne 1981; Jones, Neuman, and Shyne 19.76; Orcott 1977. Also, P.T. Giblin and E.D. Callard, "Issues in Evaluation of Action Research: A Social Service Model," *Social Work Research and Abstracts* 16, no. 4 (winter 1980).

13. See Auerswald 1972; Carter and McGoldrick 1980.

14. See Birt 1956; Epstein and Shainline 1974; Morse et al. 1977; Rabin, Sens, and Rosenbaum 1982.

15. See Morse et al. 1977, p. 613–14.

16. See Billingsley 1969, p. 572.

17. See Berstche and Clark 1981, pp. 2, 5.

18. See Powell 1980.

Resource Directory: Organizations/ Publications/Training

Child Welfare League of America, Permanent Families for Children, 67 Irving Place, New York, New York 10003   (212) 254–7410
Publishes a newsletter, *Permanency Report,* and other publications. Has a loan fund for family preservation programs.

Children's Defense Fund, 122 C Street, N.W., Washington, D.C. 20001   (202) 628–8787
Publishes a newsletter, *CDF Reports,* and other publications. .

Community Program Innovations, P.O. Box 2066, Danvers, Masschusetts 01923   (617) 774–0815
Publishes a newsletter and provides training and consultation to agencies working with multiproblem families.

Edna McConnell Clark Foundation, Office of Communications, 250 Park Avenue, New York, New York 10017
Publishes *Keeping Families Together: The Case for Family Preservation* (1985), which is available, free of charge, by requesting it in writing. Include a self-addressed mailing label.

Family Resource Coalition, 230 North Michigan Avenue, Suite 1625, Chicago, Illinois 60601   (312) 726–4750
Publishes a newsletter, *Family Resource Coalition Report,* and other publications. Sponsors conferences and workshops.

Family Service Association of America, 44 East 23rd Street, New York, New York 10010   (212) 674–6100
Publishes journals and books.

National Council on Family Relations, 1910 West County Road B, Suite 147, St. Paul, Minnesota 55113   (612) 633–6933
Publishes a newsletter, journals, and books.

National Resource Center on Family Based Services, University of Iowa School of Social Work, N118 Oakdale Hall, Iowa City, Iowa 52242 (319) 353–5076
Publishes a newsletter, *Prevention Report,* and other publications. Provides training and consultation.

Urban Family Institute, 341 Neponset Avenue, Dorchester, Massachusetts 02122 (617) 825–3317
Provides training to clinicians working with multiproblem families.

Annotated Bibliography

Alexander, James F. "Behavior Modification and Delinquent Youth." In *Behavior Modification in Rehabilitation Settings,* edited by John G. Cull and Richard E. Hardy. (Springfield, Ill.: Charles C Thomas, 1974), 158–77.

This excellent article discusses the use of behavior modification within a systems framework for treating and preventing delinquency. It emphasizes the importance of using behavior modification in a child's natural environment, and discusses how to involve the larger environment (family, peers, school) in treatment. The author suggests employing a limited range of behavioral techniques and offers alternative ways for family members to affect each other's behavior. The author recognizes that delinquent behaviors serve vital maintenance functions in families. Essential aspects of communication in which families require training are identified. Case examples are provided.

Alexander, James F. "Defensive and Supportive Communications in Normal and Deviant Families." *Journal of Consulting and Clinical Psychology* 40, no. 2 (April 1973):223–31.

Twenty-two healthy and twenty delinquent families were videotaped while engaging in tasks involving discussion and resolution of differences. The data obtained supported the hypotheses (based on systems theory and small group research) that dysfunctional families would show high rates of system disintegration, indicated by defensive interactions, whereas healthy families would show system integration, demonstrated by supportive communications. The hypothesis that families interact as systems was substantiated. The study also provides information on the process through which some families adapt to stress and others disintegrate.

Alexander, James F., and Bruce V. Parsons. "Short-Term Behavioral Intervention with Delinquent Families: Impact on Family Process and Recidivism." *Journal of Abnormal Psychology* 81, no. 3 (June 1973):219–25.

This article describes a short-term behavioral intervention program designed to increase family reciprocity, communication clarity, and contingency contracting for delinquent youth and their families. Results showed that forty-six families had improved significantly in the preceding measures when therapy was completed and that the families had significantly lower recidivism rates at follow-up when compared to thirty families receiving other forms of family therapy and fifty-two families who did not receive treatment.

Aponte, Harry J. "Anatomy of a Therapist." In *Family Therapy Full Length Case Studies,* edited by Peggy Papp. (New York: Gardner Press, 1977), 101–16.

> An account of Aponte's interview with a poor, underorganized black family. He describes his observations at the interview and his opinions after reviewing a videotape of the session. The article offers both a personal and a theoretical account of a therapist's brief intervention with an underorganized family.

Aponte, Harry J. "The Family-School Interview: An Eco-Structural Approach." *Family Process* 15, no. 3 (Sept. 1976a):303–11.

> Aponte describes his intervention with a child, family, and school. He considers the structure of each system and the relationship between the systems in regard to the issue presented by the identified client. The case study illustrates the successful use of the eco-structural approach to resolve school-related problems. This approach can be usefully employed when a school refers a child to a mental health center for treatment, yet the family has no problem with the child at home. The importance of perceiving a client in his or her ecological context is emphasized.

Aponte, Harry J. "Underorganization in the Poor Family." In *Family Therapy: Theory and Practice,* edited by Philip J. Guerin, Jr. (New York: Gardner Press, 1976b), 432–48.

> Aponte discusses the internal organizational problems of poor families; he calls this characteristic underorganization rather than disorganization. He considers the structural patterns concerning alignments, boundaries, and power distributions in healthy and underorganized families. He also describes the family's role and position in its social context and discusses the problems it experiences in its social network. An interview with an underorganized poor family is included. Highly recommended.

Auerswald, E. "Families, Change, and the Ecological Perspective." In *The Book of Family Therapy,* edited by Andrew Ferber, Marilyn Mendelsohn, and Augustus Napier. (Boston: Houghton Mifflin, 1972), 684–705.

> The author emphasizes that our service delivery systems are based on linear thinking that makes assessment and treatment of problems impossible. If an individual is labeled as depressed, he or she receives services only for the depression. This cause-and-effect type of thinking is linear, not systemic. The author believes that the present system of service provision must be totally reoriented if it is to take into account the interface between the individual and the environment. Auerswald describes how he uses an "intersystems conference" to effectively assess and treat families.

Auerswald, Edgar H. "Interdisciplinary versus Ecological Approach." *Family Process* 7, no. 2 (Sept. 1968):202–15.

After examining an interdisciplinary versus an ecological approach, the author favors the latter. He points out that the interdisciplinary approach considers the viewpoints of each team member representing a particular discipline, and fails to consider the interface between disciplines. An ecological approach focuses on the interface and communication between disciplines. It is holistic and, unlike the interdisciplinary approach, its goal is to provide a comprehensive, not fragmented, service. The advantages of an ecological systems approach and the disadvantages of an interdisciplinary approach are highlighted. An excellent case example illustrates the concepts. Highly recommended.

Barnhill, Laurence R. "Healthy Family Systems." *The Family Coordinator* 28, no. 1 (Jan. 1979):94–100.

Based on a review of the literature, the author presents eight major characteristics of healthy family functioning. Barnhill points out that the particular style of a family therapist determines where he or she enters a family system. The points of entry of well-known family therapists are described. The importance of studying healthy families is also stressed. Highly recommended.

Bertsche, Jon, and Frank Clark. "Improving the Utilization of Informal Helping Systems." *Sharing* 5, no. 2 (Jan./Feb. 1981):2, 5.

A two-year research and demonstration project designed to increase the use of informal helping networks is described. A number of studies indicate that the formal professional services that serve families rarely take advantage of informal community resources. The authors explain the advantages of using such resources and stress the importance of combining formal and informal resources.

Billingsley, Andrew. "Family Functioning in the Low-Income Black Community." *Social Casework* 50, no. 10 (Dec. 1969):563–72.

The author presents several studies that dispute the results of descriptions by a number of white social scientists of the disintegration of family life in the black community. Studies reviewed by the author strongly substantiate the importance of the family in the black community. They contend that the natural helping networks in black communities (such as depending on friends, relatives, and neighbors) are prevalent and help improve family functioning. The author recommends that social service programs and intervention techniques be based on the strengths inherent in black families. Highly recommended.

Birt, Charles J. "Family-Centered Project of St. Paul." *Social Work* 1, no. 4 (Oct. 1956):41–47.

A fascinating account of a cooperative venture, undertaken from 1947 to 1957 by agencies in St. Paul, Minnesota, that focused on improving treatment for multiproblem families. The venture was based on a study showing that six percent of families accounted for fifty percent of the social services in the city of St. Paul. Many agencies had been working concurrently with these families for a long time, but service provision was fragmented, crisis-oriented, individually-focused, and based on the presenting symptom. To provide comprehensive treatment, five agencies designated workers to specifically serve this population. These workers maintained a family approach, rather than an individual approach. Services were provided in the families' homes, and the social workers served as a bridge between the families and community resources.

The Family-Centered Project of St. Paul was the first research and treatment project to focus on multiproblem families. Its experiences provided many important insights and enhanced treatment efficacy for this population.

Bronfenbrenner, Urie. "Children and Families: 1984?" *Society* 18, no. 2 (Jan./Feb. 1981):38–41.

The author believes that two principles are intrinsic to the healthy development of children. First, a child must be totally involved with at least one adult. Second, the value of parenthood must be endorsed by supportive public policies. Judging by the types of support services offered, the United States (unlike other countries) places little value on parenthood. Families must prove they desperately need services before they can receive assistance. The author maintains that in the policies of other nations all citizens are entitled to family support services and strengthening families is emphasized rather than intervening when they are disintegrating. Bronfenbrenner warns that unless U.S. policies change, social problems will continue to increase.

Brown, Gordon E., ed. *The Multi-Problem Dilemma: A Social Research Demonstration with Multi-Problem Families*. (Metuchen, N.J.: The Scarecrow Press, 1968).

This book is a collection of articles that describe and analyze a research project in Chemung County, New York, which operated from November, 1961, to May, 1964. The project compared the effects of intensive casework with fifty multiproblem families to the provision of normal public assistance to fifty similar families. The researchers concluded that there was little difference in progress between the control group and the experimental group. According to Brown, this finding must be evaluated in the context of the project, which defined "intensive" casework as one visit every two weeks. The author questions whether such service provision can be called intensive.

Bryce, Marvin. *Family Support Programs for Troubled Juveniles*. (Chicago: The School of Social Service Administration, The University of Chicago, September, 1981).

Bryce presents a quick overview of home-based, family-centered service. The history of the movement is described, the principles of the service are delineated, and the advantages are outlined. The author discusses the types of families who can benefit from home-based, family-centered services. He also describes how to develop a program, and whether it should be operated directly by a public agency or purchased with public money from a private agency. Such issues as public education, staff recruitment, staff training, and supervision are addressed, and the author reviews eight programs as examples. The research on home-based, family-centered services is summarized, and ethical and policy issues are considered.

Bryce, Marvin, and June C. Lloyd, eds. *Treating Families in the Home: An Alternative to Placement.* (Springfield, Ill.: Charles C Thomas, 1981).
A valuable resource on home-based, family-centered services, this book contains contributions from experts in the field. The contributions are based on papers presented at the Second National Symposium on Home-Based Services, held in Iowa in 1979. The development of the home-based movement is discussed, and the book also includes chapters on such topics as working with the extended family, the use of bonding, and using a behavioral model to shape parent-child interactions. In addition, the book contains descriptions of programs dealing with specific populations, such as families with disturbed children, adolescents, and children with cancer.

Buell, Bradley, and Associates. *Community Planning for Human Services.* (New York: Columbia University Press, 1952).
This book presents the results of a research project that examined four types of problems to which community services were geared; dependency, ill-health, maladjustment, and recreational need. The book examines the nature of each of these problems, the services needed in the community, and the agencies offering the services. The research project undertook a comprehensive study of the literature on each of the problem areas, analyzed the way community services were organized, and compiled a statistical study of the four service areas in St. Paul, Minnesota, a typical U.S. city. The most interesting finding of the study was that six percent of the families in St. Paul used more than half of the city's services, which indicated that services were fragmented and often duplicated.

Burt, Marvin, R. "The Comprehensive Emergency Services System: Expanding Services to Children and Families." *Children Today* 5, no. 2 (March–April 1976a):2–5.
In 1971, a study in Tennessee revealed that the services provided by public and private agencies for neglected, abused, and dependent children were fragmented and duplicated, with no single agency responsible for service coordination. Services did not respond to the needs of children and their families. As a result of this study, a Comprehensive Emergency Services (CES) System was established. Services were coordinated, new service options were developed, and the existing programs were expanded. The emergency services initiated included emergency intake twenty-four hours a day, seven days a week, an emergency caretaker service; an emergency homemaker service; emergency foster homes; an emergency family shelter; an older children's shelter; and outreach and follow-through services. The article reviews the history of this program and describes its organizational structure. The author shows how the program provided more effective services and saved money. A case example illustrates how a family was handled by social service agencies before and after the implementation of CES.

Burt, Marvin R. "Final Results of the Nashville Comprehensive Emergency

Services Project." *Child Welfare 55*, no. 9 (Nov. 1976b):661–64.

A report on the results of the Nashville Comprehensive Emergency Services Project, a program that coordinated services for abused and neglected children. The results indicate that placement can be reduced by providing integrated service to families. The project offered emergency intake twenty-four hours a day, seven days a week; emergency caretaker services; twenty-four-hour homemaker services; emergency foster homes for temporary use; an emergency family shelter; and a shelter for older abused and neglected youth. It also coordinated placement decisions made by the juvenile court and Department of Social Services.

The article describes the impressive success of the project: a decrease in the number of children removed from their homes and in the number of children institutionalized. The program was also substantially cheaper than the system previously used.

Butehorn, Loretta. "A Plan for Identifying Priorities in Treating Multiproblem Families." *Child Welfare 57*, no. 6 (June 1978):365–72.

The author analyzes the two levels on which the evaluation of a family system takes place: one is determining how family structure enables the family to meet its needs, and the second is considering the processes through which these needs are met. The elements comprising family structure—self-concept, roles, rules, and boundaries—are considered, and the author also examines three components of family processes—communicating, parenting, and coping.

Butehorn recommends that systems concepts be employed to assess a multiproblem family. She proposes specific evaluation questions that translate systems theory into practice and enable a therapist to understand the structure and processes of this type of family. Methods for obtaining answers to evaluation questions are also suggested.

Cade, Brian. "Therapy with Low Socio-Economic Families." *Social Work Today 6*, no. 5 (May 29, 1975):142–45.

This article contains some useful, concrete, straightforward suggestions for providing family therapy to low-income families who have limited verbal abilities, poor problem-solving skills, and difficulty achieving insight. The author focuses on how these families can enhance their own resources. He believes that teaching families more effective communication skills and having them practice these skills while addressing their day-to-day problems is the major focus of therapy. He also believes that using action techniques, such as changing seating arrangements or role playing, is especially effective.

Carter, Elizabeth A., and Monica McGoldrick, eds. *The Family Life Cycle: A Framework for Family Therapy*. (New York: Gardner Press, 1980).

This book provides a conceptual overview of the family life cycle along with a discussion of its stages, and addresses special issues in families and family therapy. The book includes one chapter on the family life cycle of the multiproblem, poor family and one chapter on the Mexican-American family. Highly recommended.

Cautley, Patricia W. *The Home and Community Treatment Process: Helping Families Change.* (Madison, Wisc.: Home and Community Treatment, Mendota Mental Health Institute, November, 1979).

Cautley provides a comprehensive overview of the Home and Community Treatment Program of Mendota Mental Health Institute. Intake, assessment, treatment, monitoring and evaluation, termination, and follow-up are considered in depth. Three programs that have adapted Mendota's approach are also discussed.

Cautley, Patricia W. "Treating Dysfunctional Families at Home." *Social Work* 25, no. 5 (Sept. 1980):380–86.

Cautley presents a review of Project OPT (Optimal Planning for Children), an intensive, short-term (eight to twelve weeks) treatment program for dysfunctional families in Wisconsin. The project, which began in 1976, was intended to test whether short-term family treatment could prevent foster care. Most referrals came from the Department of Social Services and from school social workers. To be eligible for services, all of the family members had to agree to participate, and children had to be under age eleven. Thirty-two families took part in the project; seventeen were single-parent families. Treatment was provided two to four times a week (one-and-a-half hours per session), and focused on teaching parents techniques of child management.

The article also describes the comprehensive evaluation conducted by Project OPT to determine program efficacy. Program staff recommended that treatment should continue longer than eight to twelve weeks. They also outlined the qualities that contributed to successful treatment, including being supportive and providing a family with hope, developing clear goals for treatment sessions, working from a systems perspective, being able to communicate well with children, and understanding the stages of child development.

Cautley, Patricia W., and Mary Beth Plane. *Facilitating Family Change: A Look at Four Agencies Working Intensively with Families.* (Madison, Wisc.: Wisconsin Department of Health and Social Services, Division of Community Services, May, 1983).

A comprehensive review and evaluation is given of four Wisconsin agencies that work intensively with families: Home and Community Treatment at Mendota Mental Health Institute; Family and Community Services, an outpatient outreach program at St. Aemilian Child Care Center; Family Training Program, Institute of Human Design, at Winnebago Mental Health Institute; and Project OPT (Optimal Planning for Children), of the Department of Health and Social Services. The records of each program are analyzed, and Kegan's developmental theory is used to describe the families served. The process of intervention and program efficacy are considered. The authors also give the cost of service for each program and compare these costs with the costs of institutions, group care facilities, and foster care.

Chestang, Leon W. "Increasing the Effectiveness of Social Work Intervention with Minority Group Families." In *Toward Human Dignity: Social Work in Practice, Fifth NASW Symposium,* edited by John W. Hanks. (Washington, D.C.: National Association of Social Workers, 1978), 26–38.

Chestang maintains that interacting factors in a black person's family and environment either enhance or limit his or her sense of dignity. The author bases this thesis on a study of the lives of twenty successful blacks. He categorizes the families of his subjects as either achievement-oriented or survival-oriented, and describes these family types. Intervention strategies for both family types are recommended. The author suggests that the intervenor should provide emotional support, offer concrete assistance, and act as a mentor and role model.

Chilman, Catherine S. "Social Work Practice with Very Poor Families: Some Implications Suggested by the Available Research." *Welfare in Review* 4, no. 1 (Jan. 1966):13–22.

Aside from the author's condescending, moralistic tone and her assumption that middle-class values are optimal, this article offers some valuable suggestions for working with poor families. The author suggests parent education as an intervention strategy and recommends that parent groups be used to foster cohesiveness and decrease isolation among parents. The author advises family workers to reach out to poor families by employing an accepting, understanding manner. The author emphasizes addressing concrete problems and using action-oriented interventions that encourage parents to broaden their experiences through excursions out of their own community. She also recommends that parents should be given concrete awards such as certificates for their progress, as a way of recognizing their achievements.

Clark, Ted, Tracey Zalis, and Frank Sacco. *Outreach Family Therapy.* (New York: Jason Aronson, 1982).

This book recommends a community systems model for treating what the authors refer to as the low-income, culturally deprived family (LICKED). A description of this type of family, illustrated by a thorough case example, provides the reader with a valuable understanding of this population. The book is replete with other case examples. The authors view the family as part of a larger system, and emphasize the importance of working with each family in the context of the entire system.

Because the book is repetitive and disorganized, it is somewhat difficult to read. However, since very little has been written on outreach therapy to multiproblem families, this publication is valuable because it clearly portrays the population, recommends a model for outreach family therapy, and addresses staff and supervisory issues. The book's overwhelming drawback lies in the authors' strong biases—it seems that the authors disrespect and condescend to multiproblem families. This feature greatly detracts from the book's strengths. The extensive bibliography is excellent, and the authors' contentions are substantiated by references.

Collins, Raymond C. "Home Start and Its Implications for Family Policy." *Children Today* 9, no. 3 (May-June 1980):12–16.

Home Start was an exploratory project that operated from 1972 through 1975.

The project was intended to determine whether child and family development could be enhanced by providing home visitors to work with parents in their homes. The program served preschool children and assumed that parents can best educate their own children. This article reviews the project's goals and objectives, comprehensively describes the project, and discusses the results of an evaluation. It also considers how the study's findings affects family policy.

Compher, John Victor. "Home Services to Families to Prevent Child Placement." *Social Work* 28, no. 5 (Sept.-Oct. 1983):360–64.

The author believes that families can benefit from different types of services, depending on their needs. The type of service a family receives may need to change over time as the family changes. Compher describes a continuum of home-based family services to prevent placement of children, and suggests four service categories: general case management, the comprehensive social worker, the in-house team, and the intra-agency team. Cases illustrate each service category. Families are assisted in addressing concrete and psychological needs.

Compton, Beulah. "The Family Centered Project." (Paper presented at the annual meeting of the Children's Aid Society of Winnipeg, April 25, 1962).

This paper describes the St. Paul Family-Centered Project, which served multiproblem families through direct service and community organizing from 1948 to 1968. Five social service agencies in St. Paul, Minnesota, joined together to loan workers to the project. Strong community support and involvement played a major role in the project's success. A study of 150 families served revealed that 65.3 percent had achieved positive changes, 18.7 percent had not changed, and 16 percent had made negative changes. Each family received approximately two years of service.

The project had five key goals: to provide in-home services to resistant families, to focus on the whole family, to work in partnership with families to reach mutually agreed-upon goals, to emphasize and build family strengths, and to have one worker maintain primary responsibility for each family and coordinate community resources to meet family needs.

Compton, Beulah Roberts. *The Family Centered Project Revisited.* (Minneapolis: School of Social Work, University of Minnesota, May, 1979b. Photocopy).

In this excellent, highly interesting document, the author reconsiders the Family-Centered Project of St. Paul, Minnesota, of which she was a part. Her observations are extremely useful for those working with multiproblem families. Pointing out that the St. Paul Family-Centered Project suffered from lack of a theoretical framework, the author addresses the project's central issues.

Compton conveys an understanding of how multiproblem families feel and what they want. These families' need to feel a sense of competence and control over their lives is a theme throughout the paper. Emphasis is placed on using concepts from ego psychology, which maintains that every individual has a basic drive to achieve a sense of competency and power over his or her own destiny.

The author regards the worker-family partnership as crucial to effecting change in multiproblem families. She also believes that direct services will prove unsuccessful without community support; direct service and community support must be offered concomitantly. She also believes that multiproblem families require long-term, not brief, services. She criticizes programs that last only a few weeks, and maintains that families who have had a history of personal defeat and negative interaction with the social service system will require intensive, long-term services.

Compton, Beulah. *A Participant Observer's Brief Summary of the Family-Centered Project.* (Minneapolis: School of Social Work, University of Minnesota, May, 1979a. Photocopy).

In this brief paper, Compton traces the history of the St. Paul Family-Centered Project, in which she played a major role. This twenty-year project serving multiproblem families began in 1948 and ended in 1968. Although much has been written about the project, comprehensive overviews of its history are rare. Compton provides such a summary, from her point of view as a participant.

DeWitt, Kathryn Nash. "The Effectiveness of Family Therapy: A Review of Outcome Research." *Archives of General Psychiatry* 35, no. 5 (May 1978):549–61.

An excellent overview of thirty-one research studies of the outcomes of family therapy, conducted from 1961 to 1974; the majority of the studies involve a child or an adolescent as the identified client. The author found that studies conducted without comparison groups showed that the results of family therapy are similar to the results of approaches which do not employ family therapy. Studies with comparison groups found that family therapy is better than no treatment, and more effective than other types of treatment. Recommendations for future research are offered. An extensive bibliography is provided.

Edna McConnell Clark Foundation. *Keeping Families Together: The Case for Family Preservation.* (New York: Edna McConnell Clark Foundation, 1985).

This excellent publication provides an overview of family preservation services. It examines the reasons for removing children from their homes, and discusses ways to prevent unnecessary foster care placement. The book also considers the ingredients of family preservation services, which include a low caseload, intensive services, flexible hours, home visits, working with the family as a unit, ensuring child protection, and the provision of concrete and psychological services. Short-term, intensive counseling is advocated, and programs providing this type of service are recommended. Programs offering long-term (for example, one-year) services are not considered.

The booklet also reviews the legislative and financial aspects of family preservation services. Recommendations for confronting obstacles at the federal, state, county, judicial, and agency levels are made. The importance of training is emphasized, and a list of organizations and publications that deal with family preservation is provided.

Epstein, Norman, and Anne Shainline. "Paraprofessional Parent-Aides and Disadvantaged Families." *Social Casework* 55, no. 4 (April 1974):230–36.

The authors describe a year-long program that trained former social service recipients as paraprofessionals so that they could work with multiproblem families. The program's goals were to provide in-home counseling and assistance to families with severe child-rearing problems who did not utilize traditional services; to train former social service recipients as parent aides; to involve parents in an informal self-help group; and to provide an alternative to hospitalization.

The paraprofessionals dealt successfully with bureaucratic red tape and acted as role models, thereby showing families how to access community services. The parent aides' accessibility by telephone proved crucial to successful service delivery. Self-help groups were also useful because they enabled parents to share experiences and interact socially.

The project served seventeen families. Sixty-five percent of the parent aides' time was spent in direct service, and twenty percent in telephone contact. This article concludes that paraprofessionals are highly successful in working with multiproblem families. A number of case studies illustrate the effectiveness of paraprofessionals.

Ford, Frederick R., and Joan Herrick. "Family Rules: Family Life Styles." *American Journal of Orthopsychiatry* 44, no. 1 (Jan. 1974):61–69.

This valuable article explains the family as a system that operates according to unspoken rules. The authors define family rules, which can be inferred from a family's redundant behavior. Five family rules were found to be so strong that the authors called them family lifestyles. A discussion of these is provided. The article points out that by repeatedly making a family's rules explicit, a therapist can break rules that have been implicit for years. Thus, a family is helped to recognize and change its dysfunctional rules.

Froland, Charles, Diane L. Pancoast, Nancy J. Chapman, and Priscilla J. Kimboko. *Helping Networks and Human Services.* Sage Library of Social Research, vol. 128. (Beverly Hills, Calif.: Sage, 1981).

A close examination of the relationship between informal resources and formal human services is provided. A two-year study was conducted by the authors, which reviewed the literature and analyzed thirty agencies that worked with informal helping networks (all of these agencies were visited). The book's thesis is that collaboration between formal and informal resources leads to optimum service delivery. The authors examine the ways in which positive working relationships are developed between informal and formal types of care, and provide case examples. Program costs are also considered. A chapter that discusses how professional agencies can involve informal helpers is included for policymakers.

Gatti, Frank, and Cathy Colman. "Community Network Therapy: An Approach to Aiding Families with Troubled Children." *American Journal of Orthopsychiatry* 46, no. 4 (Oct. 1976):608–17.

The authors describe their work with Caucasian, working-class families within a school system in which a structural family therapy approach was accompanied by assisting families in creating supportive networks. They used a combination of empowerment, community networking, advocacy, and family therapy. The authors received referrals from the school system, and met with school officials and the family. Their work was based on the following principles: involving the entire family; initiating and maintaining contact with "significant others" (people as well as institutions) in the child's network; helping those involved with a child to view the child's behavior as human and understandable; and enabling families to conceptualize their difficulties in the context of society. Case examples concretize these principles.

Geismar, Ludwig L. *Family and Community Functioning: A Manual of Measurement for Social Work Practice and Policy*. (Metuchen, N.J.: The Scarecrow Press, 1971a).

Basing his analysis on social systems theory, Geismar stresses the reciprocal relationship between the family and the community. Two instruments for evaluating the functioning of families and communities are provided. Geismar maintains that systems theory is frequently discussed in the literature, yet it is often neglected in practice. Until the theory's importance is recognized in social work practice, a fragmented social welfare system will prevail.

Geismar, Ludwig L. "Implications of a Family Life Improvement Project." *Social Casework* 52, no. 7 (July 1971b):455–65.

Geismar describes the design of the university-based Rutgers Family Life Improvement Project (FLIP). The project's goal was to evaluate the results of social casework that served urban families by helping them obtain needed services, providing information and advice on their daily needs, and advocating on their behalf. The author examines the results of FLIP and eight other experimental control studies that served families, and makes recommendations for policy and practice. An excellent overview, comparing and contrasting these studies, is offered.

Geismar, Ludwig L., and Jane Krisberg. *The Forgotten Neighborhood: Site of an Early Skirmish in the War on Poverty*. (Metuchen, N.J.: The Scarecrow Press, 1967).

This excellent book documents the results of the New Haven Neighborhood Improvement Project (NIP), which was conducted with multiproblem and non-multiproblem families in the 1960s at Farnum Courts, a small, low-income housing project in New Haven, Connecticut. The community was ethnically mixed: forty-nine percent Caucasian (fifty-eight percent Italian), forty-one percent black, and ten percent Puerto Rican. This demonstration project provided intensive outreach casework, group work, and community organizing for the families of Farnum Courts.

Thirty of the most disorganized families received services for a minimum of eighteen months, and were evaluated using an experimental control study. The study showed that NIP significantly improved the social functioning of families; only four families showed either no movement or negative movement. The authors point out that this outcome should be evaluated in light of the fact that a small number of families were served (thirty families in the treatment group and fifty-one in the control group) and that there were problems matching the experimental and control cases. It is interesting to note that the study indicated that the greatest gains occurred in the first six months of treatment.

The authors thoroughly understand multiproblem families. Geismar's involvement in this project and in the St. Paul Family-Centered Project enables him to make valuable comparisons between the two projects (both employed the same method of evaluation). Although the St. Paul Family-Centered Project did not provide the group work and neighborhood organizing offered by NIP, the two projects were similar. More research must be done to determine whether the group work and neighborhood organizing accounted for the more extensive improvements of families in NIP as compared to those in St. Paul.

Geismar, L.L., and Michael A. La Sorte. *Understanding the Multi-Problem Family: A Conceptual Analysis and Exploration in Early Identification.* (New York: Association Press, 1964).
This book is mandatory reading. It defines the multiproblem family, discusses problems of identification and measurement, compares stable and multiproblem families, and examines the factors associated with family disorganization. Recommendations for future research and services are included. The book combines research findings with clear, concrete recommendations for action.

Germain, Carel B., ed. *Social Work Practice: People and Environments An Ecological Perspective.* (New York: Columbia University Press, 1979).
This book substantiates the theory that social workers must consider their clients' environment when providing treatment. More and more, an ecological perspective is being accepted across a variety of disciplines. The fourteen individuals who contributed to this volume are united in the importance they place on maintaining an ecological perspective. The book's central thesis is that social workers need to help their clients grow by enabling them to alter their environment to meet their needs. A number of chapters provide useful perspectives on working with multiproblem families.

Gilbert, Richard, Andrew Christensen, and Gayla Margolin. "Patterns of Alliances in Nondistressed and Multiproblem Families." *Family Process* 23, no. 1 (March 1984):75–87.
This article presents an empirical examination of the differences between nondistressed and multiproblem families in a few designated areas. Although the sample size is small, the authors' findings are nevertheless important. Two results of the study substantiate structural theory. Members of multiproblem families give each other very little interpersonal support, which weakens their ability to adapt to internal and external difficulties. This type of family has a weak marital alliance and lacks a knowledgeable parental subsystem to guide it through concrete and interpersonal matters. One result of this study did not support structural theory, which maintains that the mother-child dyad provides support for

mother when there is marital dissatisfaction. Instead, this study found that the mother's stress was focused on the mother-child dyad.

The authors point out that most of the family systems research measures specific aspects of family process, but fails to examine the family's interpersonal organization. Research is needed in this area.

Glasser, William. *Reality Therapy: A New Approach to Psychiatry.* (New York: Harper and Row, 1965).

This book's premise is that anyone requiring psychiatric treatment is unable to meet his or her basic needs. Such clients deny reality and develop ineffective ways to cope. Glasser calls these individuals irresponsible. To be responsible, a person must meet his or her needs, and do so in a manner that does not prevent others from meeting their needs. The goal of therapy is to help clients face reality and learn to meet their needs effectively.

In reality therapy, developing a relationship with a client is the most crucial aspect of treatment. By becoming very involved with a client in a caring way, the therapist helps the client face reality and recognize that his or her behavior is unrealistic and irresponsible. Reality therapy focuses on the present as opposed to the past, and emphasizes behavior, not attitudes.

Glasser describes the principles of reality therapy, explains the differences between reality therapy and conventional therapy, and describes how to apply reality therapy to a variety of situations. Highly recommended.

Glick, Ira D., and Jay Haley. *Family Therapy and Research: An Annotated Bibliography of Articles and Books Published 1950–1970.* (New York: Grune and Stratton, 1971).

An excellent reference that lists family therapy and research publications from 1950 through 1970.

Goldstein, Harriet. "Providing Services to Children in Their Own Homes: An Approach That Can Reduce Foster Placement." *Children Today* 2, no. 4 (July–Aug. 1973):2–7.

The Association for Jewish Children of Philadelphia recognized that a number of families had repeated contact with social service agencies during crises and did not respond to traditional services. Goldstein describes the approach developed by the association. It emphasizes providing services to children in their own homes and fostering family strengths, with the agency serving as the family's extended family. The approach was based on the assumption that "parenting" parents, by teaching and helping them on a day-to-day basis and enhancing their self-esteem, increases their ability to nurture their children. Staff were available twenty-four hours a day, and the program offered extensive volunteer services to parents and children. Teaching parents how to access and use community resources was strongly emphasized.

Families in the program had more than one child in need of intensive service. Fifty-one percent received public assistance or had annual incomes under $5,000. Sixty-one percent were single-parent families, and most were isolated and lacked support systems. As a result of the program, less than five percent of the children served required placement. Long-term service (three to six years) was inevitable due to multiple problems of families. Services provided cost $1,000 per child.

Gray, Sylvia Sims, Ann Hartman, and Ellen S. Saalberg, eds. *Empowering the Black Family: A Roundtable Discussion with Ann Hartman, James Leigh, Jacquelynn Moffett, Elaine Pinderhughes, Barbara Solomon, and Carol Stack.* (Ann Arbor, Mich.: National Child Welfare Training Center, The University of Michigan, School of Social Work, 1985).
This publication is the result of a two-day seminar held in June, 1984, by the National Child Welfare Training Center. The book contains chapters by each participant and a roundtable discussion led by Dr. Hartman. The contributors discuss issues relevant to preventive services for black families and children.

Haley, Jay. *Leaving Home.* (New York: McGraw-Hill, 1980).
This invaluable book examines the issues that arise when youngsters leave home. Often, many problems manifest at this time. If the problems are severe, they may prevent a youth from attaining normal adult life and keep parents from their next developmental stage, in which they are emancipated from their children. Haley offers specific suggestions for handling such problems, and provides case examples.

Halper, Gertrude, and Mary Ann Jones. *Serving Families at Risk of Dissolution: Public Preventive Services in New York City.* (New York: The City of New York Human Resources Administration, February, 1981).
This report describes the experiences, outcome, and evaluation of the Bronx Preventive Services Demonstration Project, which was conducted to see whether comprehensive, intensive services to families at risk of separation could prevent placement and improve families' lives. All of the families served lived in the Bronx and most were black (forty-six percent) or Hispanic (forty-two percent).
    Research was conducted over a two-year period, from February, 1978, to February, 1980. The sample of 120 families was randomly assigned to experimental and control groups, with 60 families per group. The experimental sample received intensive services from the project, whereas the control group received the agency's typical services. The project helped parents increase their problem-solving and parenting skills, improved the environment in which families lived, and provided "special friends" and activities for children. The primary service was individual or family counseling, which addressed concrete and psychological needs. Staff were available twenty-four hours per day, seven days a week.
    Services prevented placement for all but 6 of the 156 children in the experimental group, as compared to the control group, in which 22 of the 126 youngsters were placed. At the end of the evaluation period, one child in the experimental group remained in placement, whereas twelve youngsters in the control group stayed in foster care. The project improved family functioning in most families, although some required continued service.

Halpern, Robert. "Lack of Effects for Home-Based Early Intervention?: Some

Possible Explanations." *American Journal of Orthopsychiatry* 54, no. 1 (Jan. 1984):33–42.

This article reviews research on home-based early intervention programs that serve infants and toddlers until they are twenty-four to thirty months of age. According to the author, there is very little quantitative evidence that these programs are effective. He claims that measurement and sampling limitations, problems with the theoretical frameworks of treatment models, and the possibility that programs are ineffective for certain populations may account for the lack of statistical research that supports these programs.

Hartman, Ann. "The Family: A Central Focus for Practice." *Social Work* 26, no. 1 (Jan. 1981):7–13.

This article emphasizes that the family must be the central focus of treatment. On a continuum, the family is between the individual and the environment, and negotiates with larger systems to meet the needs of family members. Often, social service agencies take over a family's role in helping an individual. The author encourages agencies to work with individuals in the context of their families, and to recognize and build on family strengths.

Hartman, Ann, and Joan Laird. *Family-Centered Social Work Practice.* (New York: The Free Press, 1983).

Drawing from family therapy, systems theory, ecological theory, and intergenerational theory, this eclectic book presents a family-centered model of social work practice. The authors assess the current state of the American family and discuss social policies and programs, thereby providing a framework for family-centered practice. They also discuss the agency and case management issues that arise when initiating a family-centered practice. Discussions of assessment and intervention techniques are included.

Heying, Kenneth R. "Family-Based, In-Home Services for the Severely Emotionally Disturbed Child." *Child Welfare* 64, no. 5 (Sept.–Oct. 1985):519–27.

The San Diego Center for Children, a multiservice agency in California, initiated an in-home, family-centered program in 1981 to prevent placement and to reunite severely emotionally disturbed youngsters (age four to seventeen) and their families. The author reviews the program, discusses its referral and admission criteria, and describes the program's approach, theoretical orientation, staffing, and funding. The short-term results indicate that the program is successfully preventing placement and reunifying families and that it is more cost-effective than out-of-home placement.

Hill, Robert B. *The Strengths of Black Families.* (New York: Emerson Hall, 1971).

Hill believes that emphasizing the strengths of black families, instead of focusing on their weaknesses, increases the possibility of solutions. He identifies five strengths that characterize black families: family role adaptability, powerful kinship bonds, a strong orientation toward work, a strong religious orientation, and a high predilection for achievement. The author recommends that human service programs take these assets into account to improve program efficacy.

Hobbs, Nicholas, Paul R. Dokecki, Kathleen V. Hoover-Dempsey, Robert M. Moroney, May W. Shayne, and Karen H. Weeks. *Strengthening Families*. (San Francisco: Jossey-Bass, 1984).
This book provides a comprehensive overview of the services required to strengthen families, improve parent education, and foster the positive development of children. After examining the current status of families in the United States, the authors maintain that new social service programs are needed. They feel that communities must play an integral role in the establishment of such programs.

This book reviews the literature on child care and parent education programs, and assesses the programs' efficacy. The authors point out the need for parents and professionals to work in partnership. Major policy options for serving families are considered, and federally supported services and exemplary state programs that provide child care and parent education are described and assessed.

Hoffman, Lynn, and Lorence Long. "A Systems Dilemma." *Family Process* 8, no. 2 (Sept. 1969):211–34.
This excellent article maintains that human service agencies often contribute to the problems they were created to relieve. Through an extensive case study of a middle-aged black man and his family, the authors show how traditional service delivery is ineffectual and advocate working from an ecological systems framework. Dysfunction is not a result of individual pathology; the interaction of individual, family, and social systems contributes to dysfunction.

The authors recommend providing assessment and treatment in the context of an individual's environment. The role of workers must be reconsidered and altered, so that workers act as advocates, helping families obtain services and mediating between families and social service agencies. Workers should not assume ultimate responsibility for families; they should empower families to meet their own needs.

Hutchinson, Janet. *Family-Centered Social Services: A Model For Child Welfare Agencies*. (Oakdale, Iowa: National Resource Center on Family Based Services, The University of Iowa, July 28, 1983).
This booklet for administrators of public child welfare agencies describes how to plan and implement family-centered programs. It includes an overview of family-centered services; models of service delivery; a system for determining family needs; how and when to conduct assessments, including an overview of specific assessment instruments; personnel utilization; and the comparative costs of substitute care and family-centered services. An extensive bibliography is provided.

Jacobi, John E. *Meeting the Needs of Children and Youth in Massachusetts Communities: The Local Area Study and Demonstration Project*. (Boston: Massachusetts Committee on Children and Youth, 1968).

This highly interesting, yet little-known document describes a five-year study and demonstration project, initiated in 1962 by the Massachusetts Committee on Children and Youth. The project contrasted two areas in Massachusetts (Central Berkshire and Somerville) to recommend ways to increase the effectiveness of state programs for children and their families and to improve service coordination.

The study indicated that in both areas coordination and planning were lacking, service provision was fragmented, services for multiproblem families were inadequate, and there was no system for identifying and addressing minor problems before they became major crises. It was recommended that planning be area-wide and comprehensive, and that services be increased and strengthened. A demonstration project was established in each area to address local needs and implement the recommendations of this study.

Janzen, Curtis, and Oliver Harris. "Family Treatment for Problem Poverty Families." In *Family Treatment in Social Work Practice.* (Itasca, Ill.: F.E. Peacock, 1980), 77–115.

Although its brevity precludes an in-depth discussion, this chapter addresses a number of important points about problem poverty families. The authors thoroughly describe these families and recommend effective intervention strategies. Poverty families are considered in the context of the external systems with which they interact. The negative impact of these systems is addressed, and the importance of a worker acting as an advocate to negotiate these external systems is emphasized. The authors also examine the internal operations of problem families, including their structure, rules, and communication.

The authors recommend that social workers serve all family members to promote family cohesiveness, and address concrete and emotional needs. Suggested intervention strategies include providing in-home family treatment; ensuring the accessibility of the worker; involving the extended family; and participating with families in activities, not just providing talk therapy.

Joint Commission on Mental Illness and Health. *Action for Mental Health.* (New York: Basic Books, 1961).

This commission's study was an important step in legitimizing the introduction of paraprofessionals into the mental health system. The commission's recommendations were based on demographic data indicating that the mental health system would be overwhelmed by the growing number of people requiring services. The report recommends acknowledging the value of paraprofessionals and employing them to meet the need for services. The study also suggests a system for integrating paraprofessionals into the service delivery system. Although tedious to read, this report significantly contributes to the creation of a nonmedical treatment model by calling for a reevaluation of the distribution of responsibility for the mentally ill.

Jones, Mary Ann. "Reducing Foster Care through Services to Families." *Children Today* 5, no. 6 (Nov.-Dec. 1976):6–10.

This is a report on a nine-agency demonstration project in New York City from 1974 to 1975. The project provided intensive, in-home family casework and concrete services to families of children who would otherwise be placed in foster care. Each worker in the project had a caseload of 10 families, and the average length of treatment was 8.5 months. Evaluation of the project involved 549 families; 373 were in the experimental group, and 176 were in the control group. Families were typically poor and headed by women, with few relatives available to give support.

The services provided by the project are described in detail. The evaluation found that the project significantly reduced the number of youths placed and shortened the length of placement in comparison to the control group. Savings in foster care expenditures were over $2 million. Based on the results of this project, the author recommends offering concrete services as well as intensive counseling to families in which a child is at risk of placement.

Jones, Mary Ann. *A Second Chance for Families—Five Years Later: Follow-Up of a Program to Prevent Foster Care Executive Summary.* (New York: Child Welfare League of America, November 1983).

This document summarizes a five-year follow-up study of the New York State Preventive Services Demonstration Project. The project provided intensive, in-home family casework and concrete services to prevent out-of-home placement and accelerate the return of children from foster care. The study revealed that the project did not have the results anticipated. Although the project reduced the incidence and duration of foster care, success was modest, was not uniform across cases served, and lessened over time. The most successful aspect of the program was the prevention of foster care, yet there was a difference of only eleven percentage points between the number of youths entering foster care in the experimental and the control groups. Most of the children were prevented from entering care during the program's first year.

Jones describes the study, discusses its major findings, reaches conclusions, and makes fourteen recommendations for future projects. Highly recommended.

Jones, Mary Ann, Stephen Magura, and Ann W. Shyne. "Effective Practice with Families in Protective and Preventive Services: What Works?" *Child Welfare* 60, no. 2 (Feb. 1981):67–80.

The authors discuss three aspects of service to families: length of service, treatment methods, and using contracts to structure treatment. Their recommendations are based on numerous research studies. While studies disagree about whether short-term or long-term treatment is most effective, the authors maintain that length of service depends on the number and severity of family problems, the family's motivation, and the type of service provided.

The authors recognize that it is difficult to determine which types of treatment are most effective; however, the studies they review repeatedly find that provision of a comprehensive array of services is more effective than a single service. The authors maintain that effective treatment must include concrete services as well as counseling, employ outreach efforts, involve advocacy with local agencies to obtain services for families, and be provided by counselors with case management skills who can orchestrate numerous agencies to deliver comprehensive services.

The authors note that programs serving as extended families have succeeded in overcoming the isolation and lack of support that characterize multiproblem families. In addition, the studies they reviewed repeatedly found that the counselor-family relationship plays an integral role in effective service. Teaching parents to understand child development and to improve their parenting skills are major goals of treatment. In some programs contracting has proven beneficial in structuring treatment.

Jones, Mary Ann, Renee Neuman, and Ann W. Shyne. *A Second Chance for Families: Evaluation of a Program to Reduce Foster Care.* (New York: Child Welfare League of America, 1976).

A report on the evaluation of New York State's Preventive Service Demonstration Project, which was conducted from 1974 to 1975 by the Child Welfare League of America. The demonstration project served two types of families: those with children who had not been in long-term care, and those with children who had been or were in long-term care at the time of referral. Children and their families received concrete services as well as counseling.

The project was evaluated using an experimental and a control group; the evaluation showed that families in the demonstration project benefited more than those in the control group. Intensive services to families reduced the incidence and duration of foster care. In addition, $2 million dollars in foster care expenditures were saved.

Kahn, Alfred J., and Shiela B. Kamerman. *Not for the Poor Alone.* (Philadelphia: Temple University Press, 1975).

In the United States, public policies are limited to offering benefits to the wealthy and providing services to the disadvantaged and deviant. This book urges the United States to develop policies that enhance the lives of all of its citizens. The authors believe that the U.S. government must change its philosophy about the provision of social services. They examine the services of various European nations that can be adapted for use in the United States.

Kamerman, Sheila B., and Alfred J. Kahn. *Social Services in the United States: Policies and Programs.* (Philadelphia: Temple University Press, 1976).

This book goes beyond the five traditional social welfare fields—education, health, income maintenance, housing, and unemployment—and describes programs and policies for an emerging sixth area: personal social services. The topics include child care, child abuse and neglect, children's institutions and alternative programs, community services for the aged, and family planning. The authors consider the problems and potentials of these services and describe how services are presently delivered and integrated in our social service system.

Kaplan, Lauren Weller. "The 'Multi-Problem' Family Phenomenon: An Interactional Perspective." (Ph.D dissertation, University of Massachusetts, 1984).

Through case studies, the author researched the communication processes in families labeled as multiproblem, and examined their involvement with social service agencies. The author questions the current definitions and treatment modalities for multiproblem families. A literature review considers the multiproblem family from a neo-Marxist perspective. Implications of this study and suggestions for future research are included.

Kinch, Richard, ed. *Strengthening Families through Informal Support Systems*. (Racine, Wisc.: The Johnson Foundation. April, 1979).

Several national organizations and some concerned citizens formed an informal coalition to plan for the 1981 White House Conference on Families. The coalition held a conference in Racine, Wisconsin, and the proceedings of their meeting are documented in this highly interesting booklet. The publication focuses on the ways in which informal support networks help families. The state of the family, the type of help a family needs, and family policy are addressed. Support systems such as self-help groups, neighborhoods, religion, ethnicity, and the family are also considered.

King, Charles H., and Clara Rabinowitz. "The Impact of Public Welfare Practice on Family Attitudes with Special Reference to Delinquent Children." *American Journal of Orthopsychiatry* 35 (April 1965):609–13.

This article is based on the authors' experiences at Wiltwyck School for Boys, a private agency serving delinquents from New York City. The authors' major thesis is that public agencies remove responsibility from parents, often placing youngsters out of their homes. This practice further diminishes a youth's respect for his or her parents and encourages dependence on public agencies. The authors describe how Wiltwyck School addresses a youth's problems within a family context. They recommend that public services adopt Wiltwyck's philosophy, and they suggest ways to put this philosophy into practice.

Klein, Nanci C., James F. Alexander, and Bruce V. Parsons. "Impact of Family Systems Intervention on Recidivism and Sibling Delinquency: A Model for Primary Prevention and Program Evaluation." *Journal of Consulting and Clinical Psychology* 45, no. 3 (June 1977):469–74.

A rare study of the effects of treatment on the siblings of delinquents is described. Evaluation of the impact of treatment is not limited to the identified client. A program evaluation model that emphasizes tertiary, secondary, and primary prevention intervention effects is applied to a family systems intervention program for delinquents.

Knitzer, Jane, and Mary Lee Allen. *Children without Homes: An Examination of Public Responsibility to Children in Out-of-Home Care*. (Washington, D.C.: Children's Defense Fund, 1978).

This excellent publication considers the problem of children at risk of placement or currently in placement. The authors examine the extent to which public agencies carry out their responsibilities to children and their families; consider the efficacy of laws relating to out-of-home placement; determine the ways in which federal, state, and local policies and practices do not meet the needs of children and families; and make extensive recommendations for change. This book provides a national overview of the strengths and weaknesses of the child welfare system, and offers a framework for understanding the role of public agencies in child placement. Highly recommended.

Lawder, Elizabeth A., John E. Poulin, and Roberta G. Andrews. *Helping the Multi-Problem Family: A Study of Services to Children in Their Own Homes.* (Philadelphia: Children's Aid Society of Pennsylvania, 1984).

This disappointing document describes a limited and superficial study in which in-home, family-centered services were provided to 101 multiproblem families in Philadelphia. Most of the subjects were black, single-parent families with three or more children. The study's findings are based solely on information provided by social workers working with families; families had no input in this evaluation. This raises questions about the agency's outlook on multiproblem families; an evaluation conducted without consumer input is, at best, one-sided. The study is especially disheartening because it says that, in most instances, clients either were not in agreement with or were unaware of their worker's treatment goals— despite the fact that the workers were supposed to obtain mutual agreement on the problems to be addressed. Workers failed to work in partnership with families. In addition, there was no follow-up evaluation of families after termination.

Two types of families were served; half received services as an alternative to placement, and half were referred because a youngster was returning from placement. Each family received an average of thirty-one home visits, spread over approximately 13.1 months of service. Home visits, telephone contact, and practical assistance were used in service delivery. One-quarter of the families made no progress on the problems for which they were referred; approximately half accomplished moderate gains; and about one-quarter resolved the identified problems. Five factors were significantly related to case outcome: the type of referral, the emotional atmosphere of the home, the parent's ego functioning, the parent's capacity for insight, and the parent's use of the treatment relationship. The two latter factors were the greatest predictors of client change. Case examples are provided.

Lewis, Jerry M., W. Robert Beavers, John T. Gossett, and Virginia Austin Phillips. *No Single Thread: Psychological Health in Family Systems.* (New York: Brunner/Mazel, 1976).

This excellent reference is one of few research studies that compares and contrasts healthy and dysfunctional families. Although the sample is narrow—the authors studied middle- to upper-middle-class Caucasian, Protestant, urban, intact families—the results are helpful for those working with multiproblem families. The project's findings are translated into useful tools for the clinician.

Lloyd, June C., and Marvin E. Bryce. *Placement Prevention and Family Reunification: A Handbook for the Family-Centered Service Practitioner.* (Iowa City: National Resource Center on Family Based Services,

The University of Iowa, 1984 [Reprint of 1980 ed.]).

The authors provide a comprehensive overview of home-based services that focus on the family and employ an ecological approach. They define family-centered service; analyze its effectiveness; describe who can benefit from this service; address the implications for minority families; discuss the use of a family-centered service team; talk about how to initiate services; and explain how to conduct assessments and devise service plans. The authors explain how to work with dysfunctional families by using nurturing, reparenting, teaching, training, counseling, and family therapy, as well as coordination and advocacy. Termination, follow-up, and preventing worker burnout are also addressed. An extensive bibliography is provided. This excellent document is highly recommended.

McAdoo, Harriette. "Family Therapy in the Black Community." *American Journal of Orthopsychiatry* 47, no. 1 (Jan. 1977):75–79.

McAdoo believes that traditional family therapy for black families contains many fallacies and fails to consider blacks in their cultural context. Research has focused on low-income blacks, and made generalizations about the rest of the black population based on this narrow knowledge base. Blacks not only have to cope with the developmental issues that face all families, but must also address the continual pressure of racism. When blacks lived in rural settings, they had strong extended families and church groups. Now, urban blacks still rely on their own families and their extended families when in crisis, instead of accessing community services.

Family therapy with black families has been ineffectual not only because it is based on specious research, but also because it is, for the most part, provided by white, middle-class therapists. The author believes that effective therapy requires a realistic understanding of black families and employing black paraprofessionals.

McGoldrick, Monica, John K. Pearce, and Joseph Giordano, eds. *Ethnicity and Family Therapy.* (New York: The Guilford Press, 1982).

The role of ethnicity in families has received little attention. This book provides comprehensive overviews of twenty-one ethnic groups. It describes the characteristics of each ethnic group and recommends therapeutic interventions that take ethnicity into consideration. Highly recommended.

McGowan, Brenda G., and William Meezan. *Child Welfare: Current Dilemmas, Future Directions.* (Itasca, Ill.: F.E. Peacock, 1983).

This book focuses on the problems currently facing the child welfare system. The authors also discuss policies needed to enhance family functioning and recommend future directions for child welfare services. A framework for understanding the child welfare system is provided.

McKinney, Geraldine E. "Adapting Family Therapy to Multideficit Families." *Social Casework* 51, no. 6 (June 1970):327–33.

Although somewhat paternalistic, this article makes some useful recommendations. The author points out that caseworkers can be unsuccessful in working with multiproblem ("multideficit") families because their goals are often not the same as those of their clients. A case example illustrates the importance of focusing on the family as a unit and encouraging communication and interdependence among family members. Family workers must be patient when working with multiproblem families, because they repeatedly test a worker's concern and make gains slowly. Workers must also recognize and reinforce each family member's improvements. In addition, the author recommends home visits and the use of paraprofessionals in service provision.

Madanes, Cloé. *Strategic Family Therapy*. (San Francisco: Jossey-Bass, 1981).
The author begins by describing the major dimensions of family therapy and the schools of family therapy. She then reviews strategic therapy and discusses its use in addressing marital problems, childrens' problems, adolescents' problems, and parents' problems. Case studies illustrate the concepts. This excellent book is highly recommended.

Magura, Stephen. "Are Services to Prevent Foster Care Effective?" *Children and Youth Services Review* 3, no. 3 (1981):193–212.
Two main models of family-centered therapy currently exist: crisis intervention programs and intensive service programs. Based on an analysis of the project evaluations of several programs, the author maintains that neither model has been significantly successful and that both are much more costly than regular services. The author concludes that family-focused intervention may be successful if it is preventive and focuses on young children.

Mannino, Fortune V., and Milton F. Shore. "Ecologically Oriented Family Intervention." *Family Process* 11, no. 4 (Dec. 1972):499–505.
The authors wrote this article in response to an article by Dr. Carter Umbarger in *Family Process*. Although they commend Dr. Umbarger's advocacy of an ecological family therapy approach, they criticize his contention that such an approach should be used only with the poor. Instead, they recommend the approach for all social classes. A case example illustrates uncoordinated services and lack of communication among social service agencies. The authors maintain that agencies place too much emphasis on psychological issues, and fail to consider clients in an ecological framework.

Masten, Ann S. "Family Therapy as a Treatment for Children: A Critical Review of Outcome Research." *Family Process* 18, no. 3 (Sept. 1979):323–35.
The efficacy of family therapy as a treatment alternative for youth is discussed through a review of outcome research. The fourteen studies included in the review had the following factors in common: a child or adolescent was the identified client, the therapy involved at least one parent and a child, and the outcome was evaluated in relation to the child's symptoms. Outcome studies of children, adolescents, and of children and adolescents together were evaluated. Only two of the studies were well controlled. The author concludes that, although some evidence indicates the efficacy of family therapy for children, em-

pirical evidence from the studies of adolescents is particularly promising. Recommendations for future research are suggested.

Maybanks, Sheila, and Marvin Bryce, eds. *Home-Based Services for Children and Families: Policy, Practice and Research* (Springfield, Ill.: Charles C Thomas, 1979).

This book resulted from the First National Symposium on Home-Based Services held in Iowa in 1978 by the National Clearinghouse for Home-Based Services to Children. The book includes an introduction to home-based services and discusses relevant policy, practice, and research considerations. Policy discussions cover the economic system, single-parent families, research, funding, and so on. Nineteen programs are described within four service categories: education, health, social services, and services for the developmentally disabled. A discussion on evaluating home-based programs is also included. This book is useful both to those new to the field of home-based services and to those seeking innovative programs. Highly recommended.

Meyer, Carol H. "Individualizing the Multiproblem Family." *Social Casework* 44, no. 5 (May 1963):267–72.

Meyer emphasizes that the only characteristic multiproblem families share is poverty. Lack of resources and repeated rejections by society make it difficult for such families to cope. The author recommends techniques for helping, including individualized treatment, worker availability on nights and weekends, concrete assistance, and the provision of group activities. Because the problems of multiproblem families are caused by a number of factors, the author believes that treatment should involve integrating a number of theories.

Meyerstein, Israela. "Family Therapy Training for Paraprofessionals in a Community Mental Health Center." *Family Process* 16, no. 4 (Dec. 1977):477–93.

This article describes a training program for paraprofessionals in Texas. The author recommends using ecological and structural family therapy approaches to train paraprofessionals to work with high-risk families under the auspices of a community mental health center. Program design, goals and objectives, and models of supervision (group, peer, and live supervision) are described.

Minuchin, Salvador. *Families and Family Therapy.* (Cambridge, Mass.: Harvard University Press, 1974).

This overview of structural family therapy is mandatory reading for both novice and professional. Six chapters present clinical transcripts from family sessions with functional and dysfunctional families; two chapters discuss how families successfully address their problems; and four chapters focus on families requesting help. Beside each transcript, Minuchin interprets the therapist's strategies and techniques. The author discusses ways to diagnose problems and establish goals for dysfunctional families. The manner in which families change is also addressed. Minuchin describes a number of ways to restructure a family and change family patterns to create positive interactions among family members. This excellent book is highly recommended.

Minuchin, Salvador. "The Plight of the Poverty-Stricken Family in the United States." *Child Welfare* 49, no. 3 (March 1970a):124–30.
This excellent article contends that the human service professional has designed treatment for the poor according to middle-class values, so that service provision is ineffectual and occasionally detrimental. Minuchin recommends using an ecological systems approach—which considers all the systems interacting with each family member—to work with poor families. He also maintains that lack of knowledge about normal development has hindered the development of successful interventions; the majority of research has focused on dysfunction.

Minuchin presents a case study and discusses the effects of the interventions provided to the family; he also suggests alternative interventions. He points out that studies of the poor show that they are involved with support systems in their neighborhoods, especially their extended families. These sources of support are typically overlooked and could be used in treatment. Minuchin recommends building on family strengths and acknowledging progress, rather than viewing a family as pathological. Although the author recognizes that intervention with poor families must be long-term, he believes that accessing natural support systems in the family and in the community increases the likelihood of family improvement and is cost effective.

Minuchin, Salvador. "The Use of an Ecological Framework in the Treatment of a Child." In *The Child in His Family*, edited by E. James Anthony and Cyrille Koupernik. (New York: Wiley-Interscience, 1970b), 41–57.
Minuchin maintains that a child must be considered in the context of his or her environment, instead of being diagnosed and treated individually. He advocates using an ecological approach to expand treatment possibilities.

Minuchin, Salvador, and Braulio Montalvo. "Techniques for Working with Disorganized Low Socioeconomic Families." *American Journal of Orthopsychiatry* 37, no. 5 (Oct. 1967):880–87.
The authors contend that when working with disorganized families from low socioeconomic groups, traditional family therapy must be modified to consider these families' communication styles, thought processes, and affect. A case example illustrates the effectiveness of working with family subgroups by first treating the family's natural subgroups and then creating new subgroups. This increases affect among family members. Another helpful approach is the use of observation. A case example shows the benefits of having a family member behind a one-way mirror observe the interactions among a family subgroup. This offers the family member a new perspective, and gives the family subgroup freedom to interact in a different manner. Changing family subgroups and using one-way mirror observations help family members understand how they contribute to family problems and how they can alter their behaviors.

Minuchin, Salvador, Braulio Montalvo, Bernard G. Guerney, Jr., Bernice L.

Rosman, and Florence Schumer. *Families of the Slums: An Exploration of Their Structure and Treatment.* (New York: Basic Books, 1967).

This excellent book is mandatory reading for those working with multiproblem, multiagency families. It examines the dynamics of families with more than one juvenile delinquent by describing a study of twelve such families (the experimental group) who were matched with ten families who had no delinquent children (the control group). A team of therapists intervened with the experimental group, and provided family treatment to the whole family as well as to family subsystems. The authors present the results of their research, discuss the structure and dynamics of disorganized families, and provide assessment procedures and methods of intervention. The book balances its discussion of theory with numerous case examples.

Morse, Abraham E., James N. Hyde, Jr., Eli H. Newberger, and Robert B. Reed. "Environmental Correlates of Pediatric Social Illness: Preventive Implications of an Advocacy Approach." *American Journal of Public Health* 67, no. 7 (July 1977):612–15.

This is an account of a controlled study of families whose children were abused and neglected, suffered accidents, were poisoned, or failed to thrive. A family advocacy program was initiated to address the environmental stresses of families with these disorders.. The program responded to concrete problems, and focused on immediate provision of assistance, as opposed to change through counseling. Advocates worked in partnership with families, and taught them how to access community resources. Counselors offered direct and intensive family contact through home visits, telephone calls, and accessibility at their offices. Advocates used their knowledge of people, policies, and community resources to support social change.

Mostwin, Danuta. *Social Dimension of Family Treatment.* (Washington, D.C.: National Association of Social Workers, 1980).

This book describes Short-Term Multidimensional Family Intervention (STMFI) theory, and explains its application through numerous case examples. STMFI is effective with families in crisis, especially families with preadolescents and adolescents. The approach is concrete and action-oriented, and has been successful with multiproblem families. STMFI draws on crisis theory, use of task assignments, behavior modification, and MacGregor's multiple impact theory. The treatment modality also encourages families to access community resources.

A therapy team, representing the family constellation, works with each family. Each individual family member is also assigned a therapist. There are two levels of therapeutic relationships: individual and group. The therapeutic process evolves within six interlocking dimensions: spatial, holistic, symbolic interaction, social, cultural, and intrapersonal. The approach emphasizes restructuring the family's life space, opening communication channels, and improving the family's stressful situation. Length of treatment is six weeks (two to three hours per week). A team leader directs the team, which is composed of students and may include workers from other agencies involved with the family.

National Resource Center on Family Based Services. *Annotated Bibliography on Family Based Services.* (Oakdale, Iowa: National Resource Center on Family Based Services, The University of Iowa, 1982).

This very useful document annotates over seventy references. It is divided into seven sections: counseling, evaluation, minority issues, networks, paraprofessionals, program organization, and respite care. Highly recommended.

National Resource Center on Family Based Services. *Annotated Directory of Selected Family-Based Service Programs.* (Iowa City: National Resource Center on Family Based Services, The University of Iowa, 1984).

This directory describes more than 130 family-centered programs throughout the United States. Program goals, backgrounds, program descriptions, client characteristics, staff, evaluation, funding, and who to contact for further information are provided for each program. This excellent document is highly recommended.

Orcott, Ben A. "Family Treatment of Poverty Level Families." *Social Casework* 58, no. 2 (Feb. 1977):92–100.

Family treatment of the poor, multiproblem family is discussed in terms of changing poor environmental conditions and fostering family growth. This article focuses on four propositions on which intervention strategies must be based. First, social service systems need to serve multiproblem families through outreach programs. Second, intervention must address generationally perpetuated problems. Third, intervention needs to focus on the individual, the nuclear family, the family of origin, and representatives of involved social service agencies. Fourth, follow-up and supportive services must be offered to help families deal with stress. A case history illustrates the use of these recommended intervention strategies.

Overton, Alice, Katherine H. Tinker, and Associates. *Casework Notebook.* (St. Paul, Minn.: United Way of the St. Paul Area, 1978. [Reprint of the 1959 ed.]).

This seminal publication is mandatory reading for those providing in-home family counseling. The authors provide a comprehensive description of multiproblem families served by the St. Paul Family-Centered Project. A focus on the whole family is recommended, and ways to approach and intervene with multiproblem families are discussed. Numerous case examples illustrate the concepts presented, and thought-provoking questions are included in each chapter.

This publication can be ordered from United Way of the St. Paul Area, 333 Sibley Street, St. Paul, Minnesota 55101   (612) 291–8380.

Parsons, Bruce V., and James F. Alexander. "Short-Term Family Intervention: A Therapy Outcome Study." *Journal of Consulting and Clinical Psychology* 41, no. 2 (Oct. 1973):195–201.

This article deplores the lack of evaluation of family therapy programs, and maintains that most programs are based on theory, not empirical research. The authors describe a study in which destructive communication patterns of delinquent families were shaped to resemble behaviors of adjusted families. Healthy changes in family interaction patterns were evident. The authors emphasize the need for process as well as outcome research.

Pearl, Arthur, and Frank Riessman. *New Careers for the Poor: The Non-professional in Human Service.* (New York: The Free Press, 1965).
This book considers different approaches to overcoming poverty, and recommends creating new careers for the poor. Having "nonprofessionals" working in low-income communities not only assists in overcoming poverty but also addresses the need for manpower in the human service field. The authors explain reasons why "nonprofessionals" are effective and describe their training needs.

Pittman, Frank S. "The Family That Hides Together." In *Family Therapy Full Length Case Studies,* edited by Peggy Papp. (New York: Gardner Press, 1977), 1–21.
Pittman provides a detailed case study of a multiproblem family. The author describes how he worked with the family, and details the process of therapy for himself and the family.

Powell, Wayne. "Strengthening Parents' Social Networks: An Ecological Approach to Primary Prevention." (Paper presented at the eighty-eighth annual convention of the American Psychological Association, Montreal, September 1980).
The author describes the Child and Family Neighborhood Program, a primary prevention program serving Caucasian, low-income families. The program emphasizes the role of parents' social networks in supporting them during the early stages of child rearing. A family's social context influences parent-child relations and contains significant potential as a target of intervention.

Parents enter the Child and Family Neighborhood Program when a child is under six months of age, and can remain in the program until the child is three. A major goal is to encourage parents to use informal resources that can help them rear their children. Twice a week, parents and their young children meet for two hours in groups of ten to twelve in a homelike environment; paraprofessionals are the primary staff. Problems are addressed, and parents serve as resources for each other. Personal networks offer concrete and emotional support, referral, information, child rearing assistance, and role models.

Prochaska, Janice M., and Ronald E. Arsenault. "Intra-Agency Contracting: High-Quality, Comprehensive Service Delivery at Lowered Cost." *Child Welfare* 63, no. 6 (Nov.–Dec. 1984):533–39.
A very interesting description of how Comprehensive Emergency Services (CES)—a program of Child and Family Services of Newport County, Rhode Island—improved its fragmented, uncoordinated service delivery to multiproblem families who were in crises caused by child abuse or neglect. CES coordinates services on interagency and intra-agency levels. To access services from programs in its own agency, CES established formal service contracts with agency programs, enabling smooth, quick, and efficient access of needed services. Each of the five

agency programs (Day Care, Homemaker Services, Family Counseling, Education and Training, and CES) is decentralized, and each unit is responsible for its own operation. Through a Regional Coordinating Committee composed of representatives from community agencies and local citizens, CES works with other agencies. The authors describe the benefits of this system to CES, to the agency, and to the client.

Rabin, Claire, Moshe Sens, and Hannah Rosenbaum. "Home-Based Marital Therapy for Multiproblem Families." *Journal of Marital and Family Therapy* 8, no. 4 (Oct. 1982):451–61.

This highly interesting article describes an Israeli project that served couples under thirty years of age, with children no older than seven, from low-income, multiproblem families. The project's goal was to prevent severe family problems and child disturbances.

The article provides an excellent overview of the literature on multiproblem families, and considers treatment goals and intervention strategies. Most programs working with this population focus on the parental function; little is written about working with couples. The home-based marital therapy program used home visits by a male-female team that met with each couple once or twice each week at their home (meetings lasted twenty minutes to one hour). As many as four times per week, the team met with each spouse individually—the husband with the male therapist, and the wife with the female therapist. The individual meetings, which lasted from ten to twenty minutes, were informal, and took place in restaurants, on street corners, at human service agencies, and so on. Each family received approximately seventy hours of direct service over an average of eight months of treatment.

Intervention techniques included modeling, role playing, and demonstration. Tasks to enhance individual and couple functioning were assigned, and successful completion was reinforced. Couples were encouraged to develop a supportive network of friends and community services.

Reichler, Robert J., Haroutun M. Babigian, and Elmer A. Gardner. "The Mental Health Team: A Model for a Combined Community Approach to the Problems of the Poor." *American Journal of Orthopsychiatry* 36 (April 1966):434–43.

This article describes a three-year demonstration project in Monroe County, New York, which began in 1964. The authors' impressions are based on the project's first year of operation. The authors recommend a total reorganization of the social service delivery system, and suggest the need for a central agency to provide services through teams in designated geographic areas. This proposal, which was considered radical when the authors wrote the article, is currently operating at the Lower East Side Family Union in New York City.

Reissman, Frank. "The 'Helper' Therapy Principle." *Social Work* 10, no. 2 (April 1965):27–32.

The helper therapy principle maintains that a person with a problem can benefit from helping someone with a similar, but more severe problem. Although the person providing the help and the person receiving the help often both benefit, reports indicate that helpers usually benefit more than recipients. The author elaborates on the reasons why the helper principle may be useful in working with low-income clients. Using this principle with paraprofessionals and students as helpers is described.

Riessman, Frank. "New Approaches to Mental Health Treatment for Low-Income People." In *Interpersonal Helping: Emerging Approaches for Social Work Practice,* edited by Joel Fischer. (Springfield, Ill.: Charles C Thomas, 1973), 529–44.

Riessman points out that a number of studies show that traditional mental health services are ineffective in serving low-income individuals. He recommends approaches to intake and diagnosis, emphasizes the importance of relating to clients, and suggests ways to develop a relationship. Role playing is recommended as a proven treatment tool for working with low-income people. Reissman also advocates having paraprofessionals work with low-income individuals, and describes the principle of helper therapy—in which people with problems help others with problems. Innovative approaches for working with families are briefly discussed.

Riessman, Frank. "Strategies and Suggestions for Training Nonprofessionals." *Community Mental Health Journal* 3, no. 2 (summer 1967):103–10.

The author discusses the issues facing paraprofessional workers: role ambiguity, their relationship to professionals, the need for supervision, developing support groups and unions, and the need for a career ladder. Phased-in, on-the-job training is recommended. Examples of the work of paraprofessionals in different types of programs are provided to illustrate major points.

Rosenthal, Perihan Aral, Susanne Mosteller, James L. Wells, and Ruick S. Rolland. "Family Therapy with Multiproblem, Multichildren Families in a Court Clinic Setting." *Journal of The American Academy of Child Psychiatry* 13, no. 1 (winter 1974):126–42.

This article advocates using family therapy in working with low-income families with more than one delinquent member. The authors describe a project conducted by the Roxbury Court Clinic, an agency in the Boston area, and discuss the environment, the families served, and treatment provided. Problems did not exist solely in the identified client; other family members also had difficulties. To achieve a long-term positive impact on youngsters, the project found that working with parents was more important than working with the children. Treatment involved in-home therapy conducted by teams. A case history illustrates the population served and treatment provided. The authors discuss the outcome of their study, which indicates that family therapy is preventive: resolving family problems prevents transmission across generations.

Satir, Virginia. *Conjoint Family Therapy.* (Palo Alto, Calif.: Science and Behavior Books, 1967).

This excellent publication is mandatory reading for all practitioners. It describes family theory, communication theory, and the theory and practice of therapy. The book is particularly useful because it provides theoretical as well as practical techniques that can be applied to work with families. There is an extensive bibliography. Highly recommended.

Satir, Virginia. *Peoplemaking.* (Palo Alto, Calif.: Science and Behavior Books, 1972).

This excellent book is written in a concrete, easily understandable, straightforward manner. It was written specifically for families, and deals with family process, issues of self-worth, communication, systems, and rules within families. A chapter on single-parent and blended families is included. Numerous illustrations make the concepts understandable to the reader.

Schlachter, Roy H. "Home Counseling of Adolescents and Parents." *Social Work* 20, no. 6 (Nov. 1975):427–28, 481.

Although the author does not work with multiproblem families, this article is valuable because it provides a brief overview of the pros and cons of in-home counseling. The author advocates in-home counseling, and emphasizes its positive effect on fathers and adolescents.

Schlesinger, Benjamin. *The Multi-Problem Family: A Review and Annotated Bibliography.* (Toronto: University of Toronto Press, 1963).

This excellent publication provides a comprehensive definition of the multiproblem family and discusses treatment approaches. It includes an extensive and thorough annotated bibliography. Although somewhat dated, this document is an invaluable resource, and much can be learned from past projects.

Selig, Andrew L. "The Myth of the Multi-Problem Family." *American Journal of Orthopsychiatry* 46, no. 3 (July 1976):526–32.

The author presents two theses. One is that multiproblem families are a myth: it is the human service delivery system that is multiproblem. The second is that it is countertherapeutic for professionals to view problems as confined to individuals and to disregard the family and other systems with which the individual interacts.

Multiproblem families are involved with a number of agencies, and each agency has its own goals. Unless a coordinated treatment approach is taken, services are fragmented and conflictual. The author suggests a few ways to provide a coordinated, family-centered approach. One way is to choose one service provider to work with a family as the "primary therapist"; this counselor is responsible for service provision and integration. Alternatively, each service provider could continue its involvement with family members, but someone could be assigned to serve as coordinator, to insure continuing communication and a unified service delivery approach. The author points out three problems that inhibit coordinating services: the limited number of professionals trained in a systems approach; the values of agencies (e.g., most professionals only work from 9 A.M. to 5 P.M., which is not the best time to see families); and the

Protestant ethic, which considers each individual to be responsible for his or her own problems—thus nullifying a family systems approach. This excellent article is highly recommended.

Sudia, Cecelia. "Family-Based Services: A Conference Report." *Children Today* 11, no. 5 (Sept.-Oct. 1982):12–13.

The author describes a four-day conference entitled Parents and Children: A Family-Focused Approach to Service Delivery, which was held in July, 1982, in Williamsburg, Virginia. The conference was intended to provide resources that would enable Virginia's counties to redirect their human service programs toward prevention. Sudia briefly reviews family-centered services, and claims that they are more effective and more economical than out-of-home placement for children.

Taylor, James B., and Martha Carithers. "Uses and Limits of Outreach Assessment." *Journal of Social Welfare* 3, no. 1 (spring 1976):47–63.

The authors report on a research study of 188 low-income clients who were assessed on an outreach basis. The reliability of outreach assessment was found to be similar to that of traditional clinical assessment. Male-female teams, composed of psychiatrists or psychologists and masters-level social workers, conducted in-home assessments. Their assessments were based on observations of families in their homes and on information obtained from public agencies. The authors believe that outreach assessment should lead to intervention in which counselors advocate on behalf of clients, manipulate the environment to benefit clients, teach clients to meet their own needs, and act as role models.

Taylor, Joseph L. "The Child Welfare Agency as the Extended Family." *Child Welfare* 51, no. 2 (Feb. 1972):74–83.

Taylor describes the work of the Association for Jewish Children in Philadelphia, which serves families whose children are in their own homes and those whose children are returning from placement. Most of the families are isolated and have no support systems. The major goal of the service is to teach families daily living skills, thereby improving their level of social competency.

Volunteer paraprofessionals supervised by social workers serve as extended family. The paraprofessionals are available on evenings and weekends, and maintain frequent contact with families. Emphasis is placed on building family strengths. The volunteers advocate for parents, accompany them to community resources, and provide support while teaching parents how to meet their own needs.

Thorman, George. *Helping Troubled Families: A Social Work Perspective.* (New York: Aldine, 1982).

An elementary text for individuals with little or no understanding of work with troubled families. A useful aspect of the book is its lengthy comparison of healthy, mid-range, and troubled families. Publications that discuss multiproblem families often neglect to provide a framework of healthy family functioning from which to assess dysfunction. Behavioral therapy, crisis intervention, family therapy, group therapy, multiple family therapy, and network intervention are recommended treatment modalities to assist families. Overviews of these methods are provided. The discussion is interwoven with case studies. The book includes a chapter on working with disorganized families and one on helping abusive families.

Umbarger, Carter. "The Paraprofessional and Family Therapy." *Family Process,* 11, no. 2 (June 1972):147–62.

Paraprofessionals can play an important role in addressing the needs of the urban poor. The author berates those who label paraprofessionals as indigenous workers and devalue their skills. He points out that the talents of paraprofessionals have been overlooked and ill-used.

The author recommends an ecological approach to working with the urban poor. These families live in a culture of poverty that has existed for generations. Their disorganization results from being repeatedly forced to confront the consequences of poverty—poor medical care, unemployment, legal problems, and so on. Often, programs fail to deal with concrete and psychological issues simultaneously. Some address only one or the other type of issue; others address concrete issues only to clear the way for psychological treatment. The author recommends that paraprofessional family therapists address concrete and intrafamilial issues simultaneously, and work within an ecological framework.

U.S. Department of Health and Human Services. *Promising Practices: Reaching Out to Families.* (Washington, D.C.: U.S. Department of Health and Human Services, May 1981).

The fifty-three programs reviewed in this booklet were chosen after an extensive search for exemplary family programs. Brief descriptions of programs that focus on informal services, special groups, parent-child relationships, and family strengthening and support are provided.

Walsh, Froma, ed. *Normal Family Processes.* (New York: The Guilford Press, 1982).

This book describes how healthy families function and reviews the research in this area. Because it offers a framework from which to assess and treat families, this book is an invaluable resource.

Whittaker, James K., James Garbarino, and Associates. *Social Support Networks: Informal Helping in the Human Services.* (New York: Aldine, 1983).

This book extensively reviews social support networks and discusses how formal and informal resources can work together to improve services for individuals and families. The authors describe ways in which professionals can use informal networks to supplement and enhance service delivery. Chapters by sixteen contributors focus on services for mental health, health care and the elderly, the child and the family, adolescents, the chemically dependent, and the developmentally disabled. The book's bibliography is extensive and comprehensive.

Wolock, Isabel, Ludwig Geismar, Harriet Fink, and Barbara Dazzo. "Three

Child Care Programs: A Comparative Study." *Australian Social Work* 32, no. 2 (June 1979):17–24.

Few studies evaluate the comparative effectiveness of residential, foster care, and in-home services to children and their families. In 1969, the School of Social Work of Rutgers University initiated a study to determine whether providing services to children and families in their own homes would serve as an alternative to placement. The social functioning of the children and families served by three programs—residential, foster care and in-home services—was assessed at intake and after twenty-four months of treatment. The results indicated that all the programs had approximately the same benefits; however, in-home services cost less than the other two types of service.

The authors point out that although the social service system, in theory, tries to maintain children in their own homes, in practice, placement is often used and provision of in-home services is a little-explored option.

Woodbury, Michael A., and Margarita M. Woodbury. "Community-Centered Psychiatric Intervention: A Pilot Project in the 13th Arrondissement, Paris." *American Journal of Psychiatry* 126, no. 5 (Nov. 1969):619–25.

This interesting article describes a pilot project in the 13th arrondissement, a low-income area with the highest rate of mental illness in Paris. Sector psychiatry was used to serve this area: psychiatric teams served designated sectors. The 13th arrondissement, which consisted of six subsectors, contained a total of 200,000 people. A psychiatric team composed of a psychiatrist, a social worker, and a visiting nurse was assigned to each subsector. The team responded to emergency situations, and also worked with difficult cases to prevent psychiatric hospitalization. The program cost half as much as hospitalization.

The authors emphasize the importance of focusing on the family of the identified client and of recognizing the social network as the target of intervention. The use of a psychiatric team (in which all members possess equal status) is recommended as the unit of intervention. The importance of working with clients in their ecological context is repeatedly stressed.

Yale University Bush Center in Child Development and Social Policy and Family Resource Coalition. *Programs to Strengthen Families: A Resource Guide.* (New Haven, Conn.: Yale University and The Family Resource Coalition, 1983).

This publication provides detailed profiles of more than seventy organizations in the fields of prenatal and infant development; child abuse and neglect prevention; early childhood education; parent education and support; home, school, and community linkages; special needs; neighborhood-based, mutual help and informal support; and family-oriented day care.

This publication recognizes that family support programs have a positive family focus, are preventive, emphasize informal support systems, and address community needs. They provide families with the information and support necessary to strengthen family life and promote healthy development.

Index

About the Author

Lisa Kaplan, A.C.S.W., has devoted many years of work and study to the field of family therapy, focusing on multiproblem families. She is director of program development and training at Northeastern Family Institute, a nonprofit organization in Danvers, Massachusetts, which operates community-based programs. Ms. Kaplan is also director of Community Program Innovations, a national training center, providing workshops, conferences, and consultation. Her latest involvement is as a clinical consultant to a transitional living project serving homeless families at NUVA, a multiservice agency in Gloucester, Massachusetts.